WORSHIP
through the
CHRISTIAN YEAR

All-age resources for the three-year lectionary

YEAR A

edited by Diana Murrie and Hamish Bruce

Contributors:
Gill Ambrose
Isobel Booth-Clibborn
Martin Green
Juno Hollyhock
Jenny Hyson
Kevin Parkes
Steve Pearce
Betty Pedley
Judith Sadler

The National Society
A Christian Voice in Education

a co-publication with
Church House Publishing

National Society/Church House Publishing
Church House
Great Smith Street
London SW1P 3NZ

ISBN 0 7151 4903 2

Published 1998 by the National Society (Church of England) for Promoting Religious Education and Church House Publishing

Cover design by Leigh Hurlock

Printed in England by The Cromwell Press Ltd, Trowbridge, Wiltshire

Contents

Ordinary Time (Before Advent)

Appendix A

Collects and Post Communion Prayers:
Ordinary Time (Before Lent)

Appendix B

Collects and Post Communion Prayers:
Ordinary Time (After Trinity and Before
Advent)

Acknowledgements

The publisher gratefully acknowledges permission to reproduce copyright material in this book. Every effort has been made to trace and contact copyright holders. If there are any inadvertent omissions we apologise to those concerned and will ensure that a suitable acknowledgement is made at the next reprint.

C = Collect
PC = Post communion prayer

Edmund Banyard: pp. 25, 27, 35 from *Heaven and Charing Cross*, National Christian Education Council, 1996.

Michael Botting: p. 69 from Michael Botting (ed.), *Prayers for All the Family*, Kingsway Publications, 1993.

Cambridge University Press: pp. 6 (C), 8 (C), 10 (C), 14 (C), 19 (PC), 20 (C), 30 (C), 42 (C), 44,45 (C and PC), 47 (PC), 52 (C), 56 (C), 62 (C), 66 (C), 68 (C), 70 (C), 116 (C), 120 (C), 124 (C), 127 (PC), 128 (C and PC: Fourth Sunday before Lent), 129 (C), 130 (C: First and Second Sundays after Trinity), 131 (C: Fourth Sunday after Trinity), 131 (C and PC: Fifth Sunday after Trinity), 132 (C: Sixth, Seventh and Eighth Sundays after Trinity), 133 (C: Tenth and Eleventh Sundays after Trinity), 134 (C: Twelfth Sunday after Trinity), 135 (C: Sixteenth Sunday after Trinity), 135 (PC: Fifteenth and Seventeenth Sundays after Trinity), 136 (C: Nineteenth Sunday after Trinity), 137 (C: Twenty-first Sunday and Last Sunday after Trinity). Extracts adapted from *The Book of Common Prayer* (1662), the rights in which are vested in the Crown, are reproduced by permission of the Crown's Patentee, Cambridge University Press.

Cassell plc: pp. 9 (PC), 28 (C), 39 (PC), 134 (PC: Thirteenth Sunday after Trinity), 135 (C: Fifteenth Sunday after Trinity), 136 (PC: Twentieth Sunday after Trinity), from David Silk (ed.), *Prayers for Use at the Alternative Services*, 1980; revised 1986; pp. 125 (PC: Second Sunday before Advent), 133 (PC: Eleventh Sunday after Trinity), from C. L. MacDonnell, *After Communion*, 1985. Copyright © Mowbray, an imprint of Cassell.

The Central Board of Finance of the Church of England: pp. 16-17 (C and PC), 51 (PC); 54 (C), 57 (PC), 58 (C), 60 (C), 63 (PC), 118 (C), 122 (C), 126 (C), 131 (C: Third Sunday after Trinity), 133 (C: Ninth Sunday after Trinity), 134 (C: Thirteenth and Fourteenth Sundays after Trinity), 135 (PC: Sixteenth Sunday after Trinity; C: Seventeenth Sunday after Trinity), 136 (C: Eighteenth Sunday after Trinity), from *The Alternative Service Book 1980*; pp. 64 (C), 130 (PC), 132 (PC), from *Lent, Holy Week, Easter,* 1984 and 1986; pp. 9, 12 (C), 21 (PC), 25 (PC), 29 (PC), 121 (PC), 130 (PC: First Sunday after Trinity), from *The Promise of His Glory*, 1991; pp. 65, 75, 85, 111, 113, 123, 133 (PC: Ninth Sunday after Trinity), 136 (PC: Nineteenth Sunday after Trinity), from *Patterns for Worship*, 1995; pp. 40 (C), 55 (PC), 128 (C: Fifth Sunday before Lent), from *The Prayer Book as Proposed in 1928*; pp. 23 (PC), 129 (PC: Third Sunday before Lent), 136 (C: Twentieth Sunday after Trinity); 137 (PC: Twenty-First Sunday after Trinity), by the Liturgical Commission.

Church of the Province of Southern Africa: pp. 24 (C), 26 (C), 50 (C), 123 (PC), from *An Anglican Prayer Book*, 1989 © Provincial Trustees of the Church of the Province of Southern Africa.

The Consultation on Common Texts: *The Revised Common Lectionary* is copyright © The Consultation on Common Texts 1992. The Church of England adaptations to the Principal Service lectionary are copyright © The Central Board of Finance of the Church of England, as are the Second and Third Service lectionaries.

Episcopal Church of the USA: p. 46 (C), from *The Book of Common Prayer* according to the use of the Episcopal Church of the USA, 1979. The ECUSA Prayer Book is not subject to copyright.

General Synod of the Anglican Church of Canada: pp. 9 (PC), 15 (PC), 27 (PC), 41 (PC), 59 (PC), 65 (PC), 67 (PC), 69 (PC), 103, 105 (PC), 117 (PC), 128 (PC: Fifth Sunday before Lent), 131 (PC: Fourth Sunday after Trinity), 132 (PC: Sixth Sunday after Trinity), 134 (PC: Twelfth and Fourteenth Sundays after Trinity), 137 (PC: Last Sunday after Trinity), based on (or excerpted from) *The Book of Alternative Services of the Anglican Church of Canada*, copyright © 1985. Used with permission.

General Synod of the Church of Ireland: pp. 18 (C), 53 (PC), 61 (PC), from *Alternative Prayer Book*, 1984; Collects and Post-Communion Prayers, 1995. Reproduced with permission.

HarperCollins Publishers Ltd: pp. 29, 117 from Joan Chapman, *Children Celebrate!*, Marshall Pickering, 1994; pp. 21, 23, 85, 105, 109, 119, 127 from Michael Perry, *Bible Prayers for Worship*, Marshall Pickering, 1997; p. 71 from Michael Perry, *Prayers for the People*, Marshall Pickering, 1992.

The Right Reverend Christopher Herbert: pp. 61, 107 from Christopher Herbert (comp.), *Prayers for Children*, National Society/Church House Publishing, 1993.

Hodder & Stoughton Limited: p. 13 (PC), from Frank Colquhoun, *Parish Prayers,* 1967. Reproduced by permission of the publisher.

International Commission on English in the Liturgy: pp. 31 (PC), 136 (PC: Eighteenth Sunday after Trinity), from the English translation of *The Roman Missal*, ©

1973, International Committee on English in the Liturgy, Inc. All rights reserved.

Kevin Mayhew Ltd: p. 17 from Susan Sayers, *Springboard to Worship* is copyright © Kevin Mayhew Ltd, Rattlesden, Bury St Edmunds, Suffolk IP30 0SZ. Used by permission. Licence No. 894012.

Janet Morley and SPCK: p. 131 (PC: Third Sunday after Trinity) from *All Desires Known*, SPCK, 1992.

National Christian Education Council: pp. 57, 59 from *More Living Prayers for Today*. Reprinted by permission of the International Bible Reading Association.

Oxford University Press: pp. 22 (C), 38 (C), 71 (PC), from *The Book of Common Worship of the Church of South India*.

The Very Reverend Michael Perham: pp. 48-9 (C and PC), from Michael Perham (ed.), *Enriching the Christian Year*, SPCK/Alcuin Club, 1993.

Mrs B. Perry/Jubilate Hymns: p. 77, from Michael Perry (ed.), *Church Family Worship*, Hodder & Stoughton, 1986.

Scripture Union: p. 31 (Sheila Hopkins) and p. 37 (Fiona Walton), from Judith Merrell, *One Hundred and One Ideas for Creative Prayer*; pp. 41, 83, 89, 93 from Peter Graystone and Eileen Turner, *A Church for All Ages*. Used by permission.

The Right Reverend Kenneth Stevenson: 133 (PC: Tenth Sunday after Trinity).

Westcott House, Cambridge: pp. 11 (PC), 43 (PC), 119 (PC).

Wild Goose Resource Group: p. 7 from *The Iona Community Worship Book*, Wild Goose Publications, Glasgow, 1991; p. 115 from Katy Galloway (ed.) *The Pattern of Our Days*, 1996.

Introduction

Worship through the Christian Year has been compiled to help those who design all-age learning and worship – both clergy and laity – to explore and implement the varied opportunities offered by the newly authorized three-year lectionary.

For each Sunday there is a brief summary of the Old Testament, New Testament and Gospel readings, ideas for a talk or sermon, group and/or congregational activities, ideas for prayers and inter-cessions, stories and other resources, suggestions for songs and hymns, and the appropriate collect and post communion prayer.

The aim of the book is to stimulate an individual, cre-ative approach. It could be that the ideas suggested here may inspire something totally different yet appro-priate for your church. This is to be welcomed and encouraged. Only those working with real people in a real church can effectively identify what will, or will not be, successful in their 'patch'.

Using the three-year lectionary

The new three-year lectionary authorized for use in the Church of England from Advent 1997 onwards is close-ly based on the Revised Common Lectionary that is already used by a number of other Churches through-out the world. Readings are provided for every Sunday and Holy Day in the Christian year.

Year A This focuses on the Gospel of Matthew. During Advent, the Old Testament reading is from Isaiah, illu-minating the Gospel readings about the coming of Christ, and the second readings come from Romans and 1 Corinthians. From Ash Wednesday to Pentecost, while Matthew remains the focus, there are some of the traditional readings from John's Gospel, during the last three Sundays of Lent and the Easter season.

Year B This focuses on the Gospel of Mark. During Advent, the New Testament readings come mainly from the two letters to the Corinthians, while from Ash Wednesday to Pentecost the New Testament readings are a semi-continuous reading from 1 John. The first readings come from Acts during the Easter season in Year B.

Year C This focuses on the Gospel of Luke, again with readings from John coming in during the Ash Wednesday to Pentecost season. After Easter, there are semi-continuous readings from Revelation. After Pentecost, Jeremiah figures largely in the Old Testament reading, with semi-continuous selections from Galatians, Colossians, 1 & 2 Timothy, and 2 Thessalonians.

As in the other years, the final Sundays after Pentecost focus on the Second Coming and the reign of Christ.

If you are unfamiliar with the three-year lectionary, it is worth carefully reading the Notes section of *The Christian Year: Calendar, Lectionary and Collects* (p. 36), CHP, 1997. This outlines a number of points that you should bear in mind as you plan the Sunday service. These are summarized below:

- When there are only two readings at the Principal Service and that service is Holy Communion, the second reading is always the Gospel reading.

- In the choice of readings other than the Gospel reading, the minister should ensure that, in any year, a balance is maintained between readings from the Old and New Testaments and that, where a particular biblical book is appointed to be read over several weeks, the choice ensures that this continuity of one book is not lost.

- Verses in brackets may be included or omitted, as desired.

Worship through the Christian Year will comprise of three volumes of resource material to match Years A, B and C of the lectionary.

Church Year (Advent to Advent)	Lectionary Year
1998/1999	A
1999/2000	B
2000/2001	C
2001/2002	A
2002/2003	B
2003/2004	C
2004/2005	A
2005/2006	B
2006/2007	C

The seasons of the Christian year
Advent

The Christian year traditionally begins on the First Sunday of Advent, four weeks before Christmas. The three-year lectionary returns to this pattern rather than the ASB model which begins the year on the Ninth Sunday before Christmas.

Christmas

Material has been provided for the Christmas Day service itself and for the two Sundays after Christmas.

Epiphany

This season includes material for the Epiphany (which can also be celebrated on the Second Sunday of Christmas) and for the four Sundays of Epiphany, as well as for the service celebrating the Presentation of Christ in the Temple (Candlemas) that is celebrated either on 2 February or on the Sunday falling between 28 January and 3 February.

Ordinary Time (Before Lent)

There are two periods of 'ordinary time' in the new calendar, the first being relatively short, lasting from the Presentation of Christ until Shrove Tuesday. There is no seasonal emphasis in this period. Greater flexibility is given in this period to the worship leader. As is stated in the Notes to *The Christian Year: Calendar, Lectionary and Collects*: 'During Ordinary Time . . . authorized lectionary provision remains the norm but, after due consultation with the Parochial Church Council, the minister may, from time to time, depart from the lectionary provision for pastoral reasons or preaching or teaching purposes.'

The Sunday (lectionary) provisions in this shorter period of Ordinary Time are: Proper 1, Proper 2, Proper 3, The Second Sunday before Lent and The Sunday next before Lent. The first three are used for Sundays that fall in a specific period of time: Proper 1 for Sundays between 3 and 9 February inclusive, Proper 2 for Sundays between 10 and 16 February inclusive and Proper 3 for Sundays between 17 and 23 February inclusive. As the date of Easter obviously changes each year, these Propers similarly chop and change. For instance, if Easter is earlier than usual, you might only use Proper 1 and 2. This may seem confusing and it is recommended that you refer to the specific annual guides that are being published. The first of these was *Advent 1997 – Advent 1998* (CHP, 1997).

To further complicate the issue, the collects during Ordinary Time are not linked with specific calendar dates, like the lectionary readings, but to the Sunday title. So in this period of Ordinary Time the collects are for the Fifth, Fourth, Third, Second and the Sunday next before Lent. For ease of use, we have grouped all of the collects and post communion prayers for Ordinary Time at the back of the book in Appendix A (see pp. 128–9). Again, you will need to refer to the specific annual lectionaries to place the readings and collects together. We have provided simple charts to show which collects and post communion prayers you should use for these services for the next three Year C lectionary years.

Lent

This period includes the five Sundays of Lent and Palm Sunday. Mothering Sunday can be celebrated in preference to the provision for the Fourth Sunday of Lent and we have concentrated on this festival in *Worship through the Christian Year.*

Easter

This season runs from Easter Day, through the Second to Seventh Sundays of Easter and culminates in Pentecost. If the Old Testament reading is used during the Sundays in Eastertide, the reading from Acts must be used as the second reading.

Ordinary Time (After Trinity)

This is a lengthy period of Ordinary Time which runs from Trinity Sunday, through Propers 4–25, ending with Bible Sunday and the Dedication Festival. As in the first period of Ordinary Time, the collects and lectionary readings do not have the same name. All dates cited are inclusive. We have again placed all the collects for this period at the end of the book (see Appendix B on p. 130).

During this period, alternative Old Testament readings are given. Those under the heading 'Continuous' offer semi-continuous reading of Old Testament texts but allow the Old Testament reading to stand independently of the other readings. Those under the heading 'Related' relate the Old Testament reading to the Gospel reading. It is not recommended that you move from week to week from one to another. One set of readings should be followed for the whole sequence of Sundays after Trinity.

Ordinary Time (Before Advent)

This short period rounds off the Christian Year. It begins with All Saints' Day and ends with the festival of Christ the King.

Resources

Many churches that have already spent large amounts of money on resources for children's work and all-age activities may be concerned about having to purchase a whole range of new resources to complement the new lectionary. The approach in *Worship through the Christian Year* has been to recommend books and other resources that you may already possess.

The following list is divided into core books which are referred to in a number of sessions and others which are referred to only occasionally. It may be a helpful guide to building up a library of resource material for use by all the leaders in your church. To save unnecessary repetition, only the titles of the core books are cited in each session.

Core books and resources

John L. Bell and Graham Maule, *Love and Anger*, Wild Goose Publications, 1997

Hamish Bruce and Pam Macnaughton (eds), *Together for Festivals*, NS/CHP, 1997

The Christian Year: Calendar, Lectionary and Collects, CHP, 1997

Nicola Currie, *Festive Allsorts*, NS/CHP, 1994

Nicola Currie and Jean Thomson, *Seasons, Saints and Sticky Tape*, NS/CHP, 1992

Margaret Dean (ed.), *Pick and Mix*, NS/CHP, 1992

Jane Farley, Eileen Goddard, Judy Jarvis, *Under Fives – Alive!*, NS/CHP, 1997

Kathy Galloway (ed.), *The Pattern of Our Days*, Wild Goose Publications, 1996

Claire Gibb, *Building New Bridges*, NS/CHP, 1996

Jan Godfrey, *Praise, Play and Paint!*, NS/CHP, 1995

Peter Graystone and Eileen Turner, *A Church for All Ages: A Practical Approach to All-Age Worship*, Scripture Union, 1993

The Iona Community Worship Book, Wild Goose Publications, 1991

Patterns for Worship, CHP, 1995

Steve Pearce and Diana Murrie, *All Aboard!*, NCEC, 1996

Steve Pearce and Diana Murrie, *Children and Holy Communion*, NS/CHP, 1997

Michael Perry (ed.), *Church Family Worship*, Hodder & Stoughton, 1986

The Promise of His Glory, Mowbray/CHP, 1991

Together with Children subscription magazine, NS/CHP

Margaret Withers and Tony Pinchin, *Celebration!*, Gracewing, 1996

Other useful resources
Drama

Michael Forster, *Act One*, Kevin Mayhew, 1996

Michael Forster, *Act Two*, Kevin Mayhew, 1996

Anita Haigh, *Rap, Rhyme and Reason*, Scripture Union, 1996

Derek Haylock, *Plays for All Seasons*, NS/CHP, 1997

Derek Haylock, *Plays on the Word*, NS/CHP, 1993

Dave Hopwood, *Acting Up*, NS/CHP, 1995

Dave Hopwood, *A Fistful of Sketches*, NS/CHP, 1996

Dave Hopwood, *Playing Up*, NS/CHP, 1998

Dave and Lynn Hopwood, *Telling Tales*, CPAS, 1997

Paul Powell, *Scenes and Wonders*, NS/CHP, 1994

Ruth Tiller, *Keeping the Feast: Seasonal Dramas for All-age Worship*, Kevin Mayhew, 1995

Bible resources

The Puffin Children's Bible, Puffin Books, 1991

The Dorling Kindersley Illustrated Family Bible, Dorling Kindersley, 1997

Storybooks and poetry

Jim Dainty, *Mudge, Gill and Steve*, NS/CHP, 1997

Lynda Neilands, *50 Five Minute Stories*, Kingsway, 1996

Brian Ogden, *Best Friends*, BRF, 1998

Brian Ogden, *Short Tails and Tall Stories*, Scripture Union, 1996

Robin Sharples, *Livewires Live*, BRF, 1998

General resource books

Edmund Banyard, *Heaven and Charing Cross*, NCEC, 1996

Joan Chapman, *Children Celebrate!*, Marshall Pickering, 1994

Christopher Herbert, *Prayers for Children*, NS/CHP, 1993

Gordon and Ronni Lamont, *Children Aloud!*, NS/CHP, 1997

Judith Merrell, *One Hundred and One Ideas for Creative Prayers*, Scripture Union, 1995

Michael Perry, *Bible Prayers for Worship*, Marshall Pickering, 1997

Sue Relf, *100 Instant Children's Talks*, Kingsway, 1994

Susan Sayers, *Things to Do in Children's Worship*, Kevin Mayhew, 1995; *More Things to Do in Children's Worship*, Kevin Mayhew, 1996; *100 Talks for All Age Worship*, Kevin Mayhew, 1997

Katie Thompson, *The Complete Children's Liturgy Book*, Kevin Mayhew, 1995

Unfinished Business, CCBI, 1995

How to use this book

 ## Lectionary readings

These are the readings set for the Principal Service in Year A and provide the main ideas and thrust for the Sunday worship. The principle on which the lectionary is constructed is that the readings speak for themselves, without a stated theme. This may mean that those compiling services come up with different thematic material. That is perfectly acceptable. What is offered here are resources which tend to follow one trend or idea in the readings; these will need adjusting and selecting according to the readings and the main idea which those planning the worship decide to emphasize. The following sections will have to be adapted accordingly but this should not be difficult for anyone used to designing all-age learning and worship.

 ## Talk/address/ sermon

These are designed as starting points, arising from the collect and readings. They can be used to prepare material for use in church, or for other occasions such as a school assembly. Further suggestions can be gleaned from looking at the Congregational/Group Activities section, as can ideas for visual aids to illustrate the talk or sermon. These can be prepared in advance, perhaps by the children and young people of the church, particularly if you have a mid-week group. It will involve them more fully in mainstream Sunday worship. But, as pointed out above, feel free to interpret or develop the readings in the way most appropriate to your situation. It would be helpful to look at the *Stories and Other Resources* section for further ideas.

 ## Congregational/ group activities

These are suggestions for activities that develop from the readings and collect. It is important that if work is produced by groups outside the main worship, the rest of the church should have the opportunity to see the results at some point. No indication has been given here as to which activities are suitable for different age groups. It is left entirely to the leaders to decide what would be appropriate. If your church has yet to experience all-age congregational activities, now could be the time to try!

 ## Prayers/ intercessions

Again, these are designed to inspire creativity and originality. It is important that anything produced in the Congregational/Group Activities section which could be used here should be, and that those leading these activities should be made aware of this.

 ## Stories and other resources

Resources already in use for ASB activities can be used effectively with the new three-year lectionary, even session-dated material. The core books in the Resources section have been widely used by children's work leaders across the dioceses. If you do not have any, or many of them, do consult your Diocesan Children's Work Adviser about them, or inspect them in your local bookshop. It might be interesting for you to note when you last purchased a new resource book!

 ## Music

Each church tends to have its own unique mixture of songs, taken from a diverse range of music books. We have chosen a selection of songs, choruses and modern hymns, alongside familiar traditional hymns, that will help you to focus upon the lectionary readings. Again, it must be stressed that these are only *suggested* songs and hymns and do not provide a complete or definitive list. Please see page 5 for a list of music books and their abbreviations.

Drama

In recent years, a number of excellent drama books have been published. We have given a few suggestions for appropriate sketches for some of the Sundays in the Christian year. Although the sketches need to be rehearsed in advance, the end result is certainly worth any extra effort.

Collects and post communion prayers

These are the set prayers for the relevant Sunday and can also be used in non-eucharistic worship. The collect for each Sunday is used on the following weekdays, except where other provision is made. *The Christian Year: Calendar, Lectionary and Collects* provides further collects for saints' days throughout the year.

Music book abbreviations

BBP   *Big Blue Planet*, Stainer & Bell and Methodist Church Division of Education and Youth, 1995

CAYP   John L. Bell, *Come All You People,* Wild Goose Publications, 1994

CCH   *The Complete Celebration Hymnal with New Songs of Celebration*, McCrimmon Publishing Company, 1984

CHE   *Celebration Hymnal for Everyone*, McCrimmon Publishing Company, 1994

CP   *Come and Praise*, Volumes 1 and 2, BBC Books, 1978

FG   Peter Churchill, *Feeling Good!*, NS/CHP, 1994

HAMNS   *Hymns Ancient and Modern New Standard*, Hymns Ancient and Modern Limited, 1983

HON   *Hymns Old and New: New Anglican Edition*, Kevin Mayhew, 1996

HTC   *Hymns for Today's Church*, Hodder & Stoughton, 1982

JP   *Junior Praise* Combined Music Edition, Marshall Pickering, 1986

JU   *Jump Up If You're Wearing Red*, NS/CHP, 1996

MP   *Mission Praise*, Marshall Pickering, 1992

MT   *Music from Taizé*, Volumes 1 and 2, HarperCollins, 1982, 1985

SH   *Spring Harvest Praise 1997*, (Music Edition) Spring Harvest, 1997

SHF   *Songs and Hymns of Fellowship*: Integrated Music Edition, Kingsway, 1987

SLW   *Sound of Living Waters*, Hodder & Stoughton, 1974

SS   Don Pickard and Alan Luff (eds), *Story Song*, Stainer & Bell and Methodist Church Division of Education and Youth, 1993

TS   Graham Kendrick (comp.), *The Source*, Kevin Mayhew, 1998

WGS 1   John L. Bell and Graham Maule, *Heaven Shall Not Wait*, Wild Goose Songs Volume 1, Wild Goose Publications, 1987

WGS 2   John L. Bell and Graham Maule, *Enemy of Apathy*, Wild Goose Songs Volume 2, Wild Goose Publicatons, 1988

WGS 3   John L. Bell and Graham Maule, *Love from Below,* Wild Goose Songs Volume 3, Wild Goose Publications, 1989

WP   *World Praise* (Music edition), HarperCollins, 1993

The First Sunday of Advent

 ## Readings

Isaiah 2.1-5

In these verses, reflected again in Micah 4.1-3, Isaiah looks to the time when people from all nations will be drawn together and when Jerusalem will become the city of God. There the peoples will look to God's teaching for everlasting peace. Disputes between nations will be healed and weapons of war be transformed.

Romans 13.11-14

Like Isaiah, Paul points to a time that is to come when the Lord will return. He challenges the people to a renewed urgency to live as those who are living in the light, putting away all indecency, fighting and jealousy. Paul reinforces the call to 'Love your neighbour as you love yourself', and encourages his followers to take up weapons that will equip them to live in the light and to fight against the works of evil.

Matthew 24.36-44

Jesus uses parables to emphasize the need for faithfulness or alertness in view of the coming judgement. He points out that no one knows the exact day or hour when the Son of Man will return. He reminds them of the time of Noah, when many were not prepared and were swept away.

Almighty God,
give us grace to cast away the works of darkness
and to put on the armour of light,
now in the time of this mortal life,
in which your Son Jesus Christ
   came to us in great humility;
that on the last day,
when he shall come again in his glorious majesty
   to judge the living and the dead,
we may rise to the life immortal;
through him who is alive and reigns with you,
in the unity of the Holy Spirit,
one God, now and for ever.

 ## Collect Talk/address/sermon

The word Advent means coming – a time to anticipate and prepare for the celebration of Christ come among us. It is a time to prepare ourselves to welcome Christ into our lives at a deeper level and as a church to pray and prepare collectively for his glorious coming again. So amidst the distracting glitter of preparation to celebrate the Birthday of Christ, let us not forget to pray 'Thy kingdom come on earth as it is in heaven'.

Have a large or noisy alarm clock on a table in the front of the church set to go off at an arranged time in the service. Build anticipation that when the time is right the alarm clock will go off. Explore what it feels like to have to wait for something special to happen (birthdays, weddings, holidays, parties, etc.). What kind of things do you do to get ready? Advent is a time of preparing to celebrate Jesus' birth. Each week light a candle as a reminder that Jesus came to be the light of the world.

The passages in Isaiah and Romans 13 talk about weapons of darkness and light. Give everyone a small square of silver foil paper about 14 cm. Invite the congregation to mould the foil into a weapon shape. Now, whilst someone is reading Isaiah 2.1-5 invite everyone to reshape their foil weapon into something useful. Romans 13.12 tells us to 'Take up weapons for fighting in the light'. What might these weapons be?

 ## Congregational/group activities

• Make an Advent wreath, placing four white candles around the edge and a gold candle in the centre.

• Place one large candle on a stand in each of the four corners of the church, where people can see them. In the centre of the church place a fifth large candle. Explain that as part of our anticipation and preparation each week a candle will be lit. Turn all the lights off in the church and face the first candle. As it is lit sing the first verse and the chorus of the song 'Like a candle flame'. Use the following response:

Leader   Now descendants of Jacob, let us walk in the light which the Lord gives us. (Isaiah 2.5)

All   **We will walk in the paths he has chosen.** (Isaiah 2.3)

- In groups think of as many different ways of creating light as possible, such as a candle, torch, light bulb, star, fire etc. Draw or cut out these shapes and then for each one think of a word which describes the kind of weapon of light Jesus wants us to use, i.e. love, patience etc.

Prayers/ intercessions

During the playing of a piece of music, invite each group to bring forward their shapes of light and mount them on a large sheet of paper.

Pray together that each member will live and use only weapons of light.

Pray for those countries where weapons of war are still used.

HOPE FOR THE WORLD

Leader   In quietness and darkness, in peace and confusion

Jesus Christ wants to make his home and meet his friends.

He is the light of life.

All   **He is the hope of the world.**

Leader   In him there is neither Jew nor Gentile,

Neither Roman Catholic nor Protestant,

All   **All are one in Jesus Christ.**

Leader   He is the light of life:

All   **He is the hope of the world.**

Leader   In him there is neither black nor white

neither north nor south:

All   **All are one in Jesus Christ.**

Leader   He is the light of life.

All   **He is the hope of the world.**

Leader   In him there is neither male nor female,

Neither master nor servant;

All   **All are one in Jesus Christ.**

Leader   He is the light of life;

All   **He is the hope of the world.**

Leader   In him there is neither rich nor poor,

Neither middle class nor working class;

All   **All are one in Jesus Christ.**

Leader   He is the light of life;

All   **He is the hope of the world.**

The Iona Community Worship Book (p. 92)

 Stories and other resources

'Advent', in *Children Celebrate!*

Lois Rock, 'Advent ring', in *Festivals of the Christian Year*, Lion, 1996

Betty Pedley, 'Advent craft activities', in *Together for Festivals*

Advent sections in *Festive Allsorts* and *The Promise of His Glory*

 Drama

Jane Phillips, 'Are you ready for Christmas?', in *Together for Festivals*

'Preparing the way', in *Livewires Live*

 Music

Christ is the world's true light (HAMNS 346, HON 78, HTC 323)

Gloria (MT 1)

How lovely on the mountains (SHF 176, HON 219)

Like a candle flame (MP 420)

Lord, the light of your love is shining (HON 317, MP 445)

O come, O come, Emmanuel (HAMNS 26, HON 358, HTC 66)

Thy kingdom come, O God (HAMNS 177, HON 519, HTC 334)

When he comes (MP 752)

Post communion prayer

O Lord our God,
make us watchful and keep us faithful
as we await the coming of your Son our Lord;
that, when he shall appear,
he may not find us sleeping in sin
but active in his service
and joyful in his praise;
through Jesus Christ our Lord.

The Second Sunday of Advent

Readings

Isaiah 11.1-10

Isaiah paints a beautiful picture of the eternal peaceful kingdom where wolves and sheep will live together free of enmity and evil, totally transformed. The coming King is likened to a new branch that will sprout from a tree that has been cut down and will be from the line of David. So clearly will he possess the spirit of God within, that his rule will be one of justice and peace. A day will come when all nations will gather and honour the new King.

Romans 15.4-13

Paul continues his theme of how the Christian life should be lived especially in the way of love and acceptance of one another. As Christ has accepted us so we are to accept one another both Jew and Gentile. Together with one voice we are called to praise the God and Father of our Lord Jesus Christ.

Matthew 3.1-12

These verses tell the story of John in the desert of Judea, calling the people to repentance and baptism. The washing of baptism symbolizes a wiping clean of previous wrongdoing in preparation for the coming of the Messiah. John's strong words to the Pharisees and Sadducees are a warning that they should not be complacent in their ancestry, but that they too need to turn from their sins. John goes on to tell of the greatness of the one who is to follow who will baptize not with water but with the Holy Spirit.

Collect

O Lord, raise up, we pray, your power
and come among us,
and with great might succour us;
that whereas, through our sins and wickedness
we are grievously hindered
in running the race that is set before us,
your bountiful grace and mercy
may speedily help and deliver us;
through Jesus Christ your Son our Lord,
to whom with you and the Holy Spirit,
be honour and glory, now and for ever.

Talk/address/ sermon

Jesse was the father of King David. Isaiah's prophecy tells us that Jesus would be born of the House of David. By going back to David's father Jesse, we get a picture of Jesus' ancestry, or family tree.

The origin of the Jesse tree probably goes back to medieval times as a way of teaching Bible stories of how God dealt with his people before he sent his son into the world. Using a large branch in a pot (or a drawing of a tree), hang up symbolic pictures of some of the Old Testament people of God.

Adam and Eve	**a tree**
Noah	**an ark**
Abraham	**stars**
Joseph	**a coloured coat**
Moses	**the ten commandments**
David	**a sheep or a harp**

Prepare someone to come into church wearing clothes like John the Baptist and shouting 'Turn away from your sins because the kingdom of God is near'. A second person could arrive wearing sandwich boards with the words, 'Turn away from your sins, the kingdom of God is near' written in large letters; this person says nothing but just walks up and down. A third person arrives dressed in a suit with a pile of papers. He/she moves to the lectern and prepares to give a speech.

Ask members of the congregation what their reactions are to the people delivering their message. Will their appearance affect what you hear? Refer to the Gospel reading, how do you think people reacted to John's message?

Congregational/ group activities

- Light two candles today either on the Advent wreath or in two corners of the church. The light might be processed from one candle to the next whilst the congregation sing 'Like a candle flame' or the 'Gloria Patri et Filio' (MT 2). When both candles are lit:

Leader There shall come forth a shoot from the branch of Jesse

All **The Spirit of the Lord shall rest upon him.**

- Invite groups to think of their own symbols to hang on the Jesse tree, which say something about themselves and their story with God. Depending on the size of the congregation each group could produce its own Jesse tree.

- Look at the passage in Isaiah 11 called 'The Peaceful Kingdom'. Discuss together what other pictures of peace and justice you would like to include, eg. the hungry being fed, families being reconciled.

- Paul's words 'Turn away from your sins because the kingdom of Heaven is near' were difficult words for people to hear, yet many of them responded and were baptized. In groups discuss what important message you would like people to hear this Christmas time about God's love. Write the words on a large sheet of card or paper to create a poster to hang outside your church.

 ## Prayers/ intercessions

As a focus for the prayers have three large outlines of trees. As prayers are read for each section invite children to stick leaves on the trees.

Thank God for his creation and pray that we might be good stewards of his world.

Leader   In the beginning you gave us the tree of life;

All **We come to you, Lord Jesus Christ.**

Pray for the times we fail to show Jesus' love, for the sins of the world.

Leader On the tree of the cross you took away our sins

All **We come to you, Lord Jesus Christ.**

Thank God for sending his Son to live among us, ask him to help us to share his love and peace with those whom we meet who are sad or lonely so they too may know Christ's hope in their troubles.

Leader You are the new branch of the tree of David bringing hope to all peoples

All **We come to you Lord Jesus Christ.**

The Promise of His Glory (p. 141)

 ## Stories and other resources

'Prepare ye the way of the Lord', from the musical *Godspell*

'How to make a Jesse tree', in *Festive Allsorts* (p. 8)

Lois Rock and Louise Rawlings, *Bright Star Night*, Lion, 1997

Nicholas Allan, *Jesus' Christmas Party*, Red Fox, 1991

 ## Drama

'The right person for the job', in *Playing Up*

 ## Music

Come, Lord Jesus, come (BBP 29)

From heaven you came (HON 148, SHF 120, MP 162)

Hail to the Lord's anointed (HAMNS 142, HON 193, HTC 190, SHF 146)

Jesus shall reign wher'er the sun (HAMNS 143, HON 277, HTC 516, SHF 289)

Kyrie (MT 1)

Make way, make way (HON 329)

On Jordan's bank the Baptist's cry (HAMNS 27, HON 401)

Peace is flowing like a river (HON 412, MP 554)

Post communion prayer

Father in heaven,
who sent your Son to redeem the world
and will send him again to be our judge:
give us grace so to imitate him
    in the humility and purity of his first coming
that, when he comes again,
we may be ready to greet him
with joyful love and firm faith;
through Jesus Christ our Lord.

The Third Sunday of Advent

Readings

Isaiah 35.1-10

This beautiful chapter is full of hope, in stark contrast to chapter 34. Now destruction is replaced by re-creation, the flowers will bloom in the desert, dry land will be filled with streams. God's people will be brought to safety on the 'Road to Holiness'. He will heal and rescue his people and bring them home.

James 5.7-10

James encourages the people to wait patiently for the Lord's coming as a farmer waits for his crops to grow. He urges them not to argue and complain among one another so that God will not judge them. Instead they should look to the prophets as examples of patient endurance.

Matthew 11.2-11

John, in prison, is puzzled by reports of Jesus and sends his disciples to find out if Jesus is the Messiah. In his response Jesus reminds John of the words of the prophet Isaiah (35.5,6 and 61.1) which he is now fulfilling, 'The blind can see, the lame can walk. . .' Despite John's doubts, Jesus speaks highly of him.

Collect

O Lord Jesus Christ,
who at your first coming sent your messenger
to prepare your way before you:
grant that the ministers and stewards of your
    mysteries
may likewise so prepare and make ready your way
by turning the hearts of the disobedient
    to the wisdom of the just,
that at your second coming to judge the world
we may be found an acceptable people in your
    sight;
for you are alive and reign with the Father
in the unity of the Holy Spirit,
one God, now and for ever.

Talk/address/sermon

From the back of the church have someone dressed up as a Town crier ringing a bell.

'Come near, you nations, and listen
Pay attention, you peoples
Let the earth hear, and all that is in it.' Isaiah 34.1

As the town crier arrives at the front of the church a conversation could take place between the leader and the town crier as to what the message is – a message of hope that is to come, a time of change and re-creation.

Talk about the things that change and illustrate with either objects or pictures or use an OHP:

A flower bulb	A hyacinth in flower
A picture of a caterpillar	A butterfly
A baby (or a child)	An older member of the congregation
A sad face	A happy face

The readings reflect a time of change, a time of waiting in hope. What kinds of things might we wait in hope for?

Have a large interesting-shaped parcel wrapped up on a table in the front of the church. Make several references to it during the service, building up a sense of anticipation. Refer to the need to wait patiently for the right time to open the parcel. Talk about waiting for Christmas and how Mary waited, the prophets waited, John the Baptist waited, Simeon and Anna waited. Open the parcel to reveal a smaller parcel inside with the message 'Not to be opened until Christmas Day' (or an appropriate day when the congregation will be present again e.g. Advent 4, Carol service, Christmas Eve). Alternatively, inside the large parcel reveal flower bulbs, enough for everyone in the congregation to take one home. Encourage members of the congregation to plant their bulbs and to wait patiently for the change to take place. Both ideas could be used together.

Congregational/ group activities

- Light candles 1, 2 and 3 either on the Advent wreath or in three of the four corners of the church. Sing verses 1 and 2 of 'Like a Candle Flame' or the 'Gloria' from Taize.

(If using candles around the church, the children could process with the light from one candle to the next until the three candles are lit.)

Leader Be patient brothers and sisters until the Lord's coming.

All **We will stand firm because the Lord's coming is near.**

- Isaiah 35.8 talks about a highway called 'The Way of Holiness'. Make reference to the *Children in the Way* report and to being a Pilgrim people. Divide the congregation into groups, with a long strip of wallpaper and felt pens for each group. Invite everyone to draw themselves on the paper. Bring the papers together to create a 'Highway of Holiness'.

Prayers/ intercessions

Use the prayers to focus the hope that Christ brings into a hurting world.

Using the Iona song 'A touching place' (WGS 3) pause between the singing of each verse and chorus to name people quietly who have come to mind.

Play the tune of the carol 'O Little Town of Bethlehem' whilst prayers are led reflecting how Christ came to change the world:

Pray for peace instead of war

Pray for the sick to be made whole

Pray for the homeless and lonely to find shelter and a friend

Pray for each other that Christ's love may live in each heart.

The pictures drawn by the groups of the 'Highway of Holiness' could be brought in at this point, reflecting we are Christ's hands and feet that can bring about change in our hurting world.

(If an OHP has been used earlier in the service use the images of change as a focus for prayer.)

Stories and other resources

Eric Cole, *The Very Hungry Caterpillar*, Hamish Hamilton, 1994!

All Aboard!

Best Friends

Alan and Linda Parry, *God's Little Angel*, Hunt & Thorpe, 1997

Drama

'The best attitudes', in *Acting Up*

♪ Music

A great and mighty wonder (HAMNS 43, HON 2, HTC 49)

A touching place (WGS 3, p.66)

Jesus is King (SHF 277, MP 366)

Jesus, you are changing me (MP 389)

Make way, make way (HON 329, MP 457)

O for a thousand tongues to sing (HAMNS 125, HON 362, HTC 219, SHF 394)

Rejoice! the Lord is King (HAMNS 139, HON 432, HTC 180, SHF 463)

Restore, O Lord (HON 434, SHF 464)

Wait for the Lord (HON 528)

Post communion prayer

We give you thanks, O Lord, for these heavenly
   gifts;
kindle in us the fire of your Spirit
that when your Christ comes again
we may shine as lights before his face;
who is alive and reigns now and for ever.

The Fourth Sunday of Advent

 ## Readings

Isaiah 7.10-16

The date is about 735 BC and the kingdom of King Ahaz is coming under attack from all sides. When King Ahaz refuses to join the Israel/Syria alliance against Assyria, they attack Judah. At this point God sends Isaiah to King Ahaz to tell him to put his trust in God rather than the Assyrians. Ahaz refuses Isaiah's invitation to ask God for a sign but Isaiah tells him that God will send a sign which will be for a wider audience than Ahaz and of more import than a show of power. There will one day be born a child 'Immanuel' – God with us.

Romans 1.1-7

In these introductory verses from Paul's letter to the Romans he encapsulates the message of the Gospel as well as his own part in bringing the Good News to the nations and sharing Christ's grace and peace with his fellow Christians in Rome. He points to the Messianic prophecy and to Jesus' coming as a descendant of David's family. Paul moves on to show Christ's holiness and God's power in raising him from the dead. He describes the great privilege of being an apostle of Christ and invites his listeners to share that calling and to rejoice in being loved and called to be God's own people.

Matthew 1.18-25

Joseph, engaged to Mary, discovers that she is to have a baby by the Holy Spirit. At first Joseph, not wanting to disgrace Mary publicly, makes plans to break off the engagement. An angel appears to Joseph in a dream and tells him not to be afraid to take Mary as his wife as the child she carries is God's son Immanuel, 'God with us'.

Collect

God our redeemer,
who prepared the Blessed Virgin Mary
to be the mother of your Son:
grant that, as she looked for his coming as our
    saviour,
so we may be ready to greet him
when he comes again as our judge;
who is alive and reigns with you,
in the unity of the Holy Spirit,
one God, now and for ever.

 ## Talk/address/ sermon

Matthew's Gospel gives Joseph's account of the promised Messiah while Luke's Gospel tells the story from Mary's point of view.

Have two characters dressed up, one as Mary and one as Joseph, and use an interview technique to ask the two characters to tell their own side of the story. During the questioning draw out possible feelings from both characters.

What's in a name? Talk about naming an expected baby and how the decision on a name finally comes about. Using a baby naming book, which contains meanings for names, find out the meaning of some of the members of the congregation's names.

Mary and Joseph were told what to call their baby and they knew he would be a boy! The name they were to give him reflected who he was:

'Jesus' – the Hebrew name 'Yehoshua' or 'Yahweh saves' – he was to save his people from their sins. 'Immanuel' – 'God with us' and 'The Son of the Most High God' were other names applied to Jesus.

 ## Congregational/ group activities

- In groups look up other Old Testament names given to Jesus. In Isaiah 9.6:

    > Wonderful Counsellor
    > Mighty God
    > Prince of Peace
    > Eternal Father

    Give each group a prepared banner made from either wallpaper or fabric. Ask each group to choose one of the names for Jesus and to illustrate the name on the banner using sticky-back fablon for the letters. At the end of the group time the banners could be processed around the church during the singing of a hymn.

- Mary and Joseph responded to the angel's message with acceptance and obedience. In groups think of ways you could show willingness to do God's will. What kinds of things does God ask us to do?

- This week light four candles either on the Advent ring or in the four corners of the church. Again process the light to all four corners of the church whilst singing 'The Light of Christ' or Gloria (Taizé).

Leader Mary said 'I am the Lord's servant, may it happen to me as you have said'

All **Come Lord Jesus and live in our hearts.**

Prayers/ intercessions

After each section of prayer respond:

Leader In our weakness

All **Help us to say yes Lord.**

Pray for times when we stand by and see injustice done.

Pray for times when in our business we fail to meet the needs of others.

Pray for times when we find it hard to respond to God by saying yes.

Using the banners as a focus:

The Prince of Peace – pray for peace in the world.

Wonderful Counsellor – pray for Christ's wisdom and understanding.

Mighty God – pray for Christ's lordship in the world and in our lives.

Everlasting Father – pray for Christ's presence with all who are sick and lonely.

Invite members of the congregation who have had a baby in the last year to come and write the baby's name on a Christmas tree bauble (previously prepared with a narrow band of paper around it). Grandparents, or children who have been baptized in the last year might also like to come forward. Invite those who come forward to hang their bauble on the church Christmas tree and then pray together for these new young members of the church family.

Stories and other resources

Bob Hartman, 'The Surprise', in *Angels, Angels All Around,* Lion, 1993

Sample choral prayers, in *Children Aloud!* (p.18)

'Christmas', in *Children Celebrate!*,

Drama

'Mary and the angel', in *Telling Tales*

'Message received but not understood,' in *Plays for All Seasons*

 ## Music

He came down that we may have love (JU p. 36)

Joy to the world, the Lord is come (HON 283, HTC 197)

Mary had a little baby (JP 164)

Of the Father's love begotten (HAMNS 33, HON 395, HTC 56)

Tell out my soul, the greatness of the Lord (HAMNS 422, HON 467, HTC 42, SHF 498)

The angel Gabriel from heaven came (HON 471)

The light of Christ (MP 652)

The Lord is my light (WP 76)

Post communion prayer

Heavenly Father,
who chose the Blessed Virgin Mary
to be the mother of the promised saviour:
fill us your servants with your grace,
that in all things we may embrace your holy will
and with her rejoice in your salvation;
through Jesus Christ our Lord.

Christmas Day

25 December

 ## Readings

Isaiah 9.2-7

Isaiah foretells a time to come when the trappings of war will be laid down and those tribes first to be crushed by Assyria will be the first to see the light and be set free by the Prince of Peace. This child born to us will rule with righteousness and justice and his reign of peace will never end.

Titus 2.11-14

Paul reminds Titus of the character of those who are to teach the gospel of Christ. He reflects on the need to live godly lives while waiting for Christ to come again. Christ rescued us from evil ways by giving himself for us. As we belong to him so we should strive to do that which is good and pleases him.

Luke 2.1-14 [15–20]

Joseph takes Mary to the town of Bethlehem where he must register. Whilst they are in Bethlehem, Mary gives birth to her son and lays him in a manger. Shepherds in nearby fields, watching over their sheep, are visited by angels who tell them of the birth of their Saviour in the town of David. The shepherds hurry into Bethlehem and find Mary and Joseph and the baby just as the angels had told them.

Alternatively, the following sets of readings may be used:

Readings set 2	Readings set 3
Isaiah 62.6-12	Isaiah 52.7-10
Titus 3.4-7	Hebrews 1.1-4 [5-12]
Luke 2.1-7 and 8-20	John 1.1-14

Collect

Almighty God,
you have given us your only-begotten Son
to take our nature upon him
and as at this time to be born of a pure virgin:
grant that we, who have been born again
and made your children by adoption and grace,
may daily be renewed by your Holy Spirit;
through Jesus Christ your Son our Lord,
who is alive and reigns with you,
in the unity of the Holy Spirit,
one God, now and for ever.

Talk/address/ sermon

In the centre of the church have an empty crib (this could either be a large size crib or the nativity scene). Ask the congregation what is missing. Draw out that it is Christmas Day, the day we celebrate the birth of Jesus, but where is the baby? Ask what symbols we could place in the manger instead of a baby:

A light	For Jesus is the Light of the World
A dove	For Jesus came to bring peace
A crown	For Jesus is the King of all nations
A flower/a star	For Jesus is the creator of the world

Make a large cracker from gold paper, using a card tube for the centre. Cut the tube in half making the cracker and pull into two halves. Inside the cracker place a paper crown, a small gift and a message i.e. Luke 2.14 or Isaiah 9.6. Decorate the cracker with a flower or stars.

Invite members of the congregation to remember Jesus in the middle of their Christmas celebrations as they pull their crackers. Invite two people to help you to pull the cracker. Talk about the different symbols that the cracker can represent.

Gold cracker	the gifts given to Jesus.
Decoration of the cracker flower/stars	Jesus is creator of the world.
Paper hat	Jesus is King of all nations
Message inside the cracker	the message of the prophets/angels.
Small gift e.g. candle	Jesus came as the light of the world

If you used the unopened gift idea on Advent 3, place the parcel in the centre of a table in the front of the church. Talk about what gifts members of the congregation have already received. What might be in this gift that is addressed to everyone with love from God?

Open the box with help from members of the congregation and have inside a candle. This could be the candle that takes the centre place either in the Advent wreath or the Advent candles around the church. Jesus came as the Light of the World to show us the greatest gift of all, the gift of God's love for us and how to share love with one another. Place the candle in its place and light it.

Congregational/ group activities

- Talk about today being a party. What do we do at parties? (eat party food, play games etc.). Ask for four teams in corners of the church. Give each team a large dice. Prepare several photocopied sheets with the words from Luke 2.14 written on them and cut into large jigsaw puzzle pieces. You will need at least six pieces with the numbers 1–6 written on the back to correspond with the numbers on the dice. Place the jigsaw pieces on a table in the centre of the church. As each member of the team throws the dice they collect the corresponding piece of jigsaw, until they have a complete puzzle and can shout out the message proclaiming, 'Glory to God in the Highest, and peace on earth to those with whom he is well pleased'.

- Light four Advent candles around the church, ending with the fifth candle in the centre of the church (refer to sermon ideas if using the candle from the gift).

- Sing 'The Light of Christ has come into the world' or Taizé Gloria. Process the light around the church.

Leader Let us go to Bethlehem and see this thing that has happened which the Lord has told us. (Luke 2.15)

All **O come let us adore him – Christ the Lord.**

Prayers/ intercessions

Have the letters of the word CHRISTMAS written on individual cards. On the back of each card write a prayer beginning with each initial letter e.g.

Come and be our friend Lord Jesus . . .

Help us tell others about your love . . .

Remind us to pray for those who are sad and lonely . . .

In all we do this Christmas, help us not to forget you . . .

Shepherds came to celebrate your birth, may we too come and worship you . . .

Thank you that you came to live among us . . . etc.

At the beginning of the time of prayer give everyone a heart-shaped piece of card or paper. Invite the congregation to look at their heart shape whilst prayers are said.
Pray for those who don't know love . . .
Pray for those who don't experience peace . . .
Pray for those in despair who have lost hope . . .

Ask the congregation to write their names on the heart shapes. During the playing of the carol 'In the bleak midwinter' invite everyone to come and stick their heart shape on a large sheet of paper as an offering of their love to Jesus.

'What shall I give him, poor as I am . . .
What I can I give him, give my heart'

Jesus asks us to share his love, hope and peace in the world. Link into the sharing of the Peace.

Stories and other resources

Sheila Forsdyke, 'The girl who saw Christmas', in *Together for Festivals*

Nick Butterworth and Mike Inkpen, *The Nativity Play*, Knight Books, 1986

Nicholas Allan, *Jesus' Christmas Party*, Red Fox Picture Book, 1991

Nick Butterworth and Mike Inkpen, *The Fox's Story*, Marshall Pickering, 1990

Drama

'The Nativity', in *Telling Tales*

Jane Phillips, 'Are you ready for Christmas?', in *Together for Festivals*

Peter Comaish, 'In the picture', *Together with Children* magazine (Dec 96)

'Christmas – All-Age Nativity plays', in *Children Aloud!*

Music

A great and mighty wonder (HAMNS 43, HON 2, HTC 49)

Go, tell it on the mountain (HON 165)

Hark! the herald angels sing (HAMNS 35, HON 199, HTC 59)

Heaven invites you to a party (TS 150)

He was born a little child (WP 28)

Lullaby Jesus (*Feeling Good* p. 7)

O come all ye faithful (HAMNS 34, HON 357, WP)

The Virgin Mary (JP 251)

You are the King of Glory (HON 570, SHF 630)

Post communion prayer

God our Father,
whose Word has come among us
in the Holy Child of Bethlehem:
may the light of faith illumine our hearts
and shine in our words and deeds;
through him who is Christ the Lord.

The First Sunday of Christmas

 ## Readings

Isaiah 63.7-9

Isaiah speaks of God's unfailing love to Israel. He remembers how, despite Israel's rebellion against God, God remained faithful to them and how his love and compassion reached out to rescue them.

Hebrews 2.10-18

These verses reflect how Jesus, in becoming human, came to share our human nature, to destroy the power of death and to free us to become brothers and sisters of Christ and children of God.

Matthew 2.13-23

Following the visit of the wise men from the East an angel appears to Joseph in a dream telling him to take Mary and the child and escape to Egypt. Herod would be looking for the child to kill him. Herod gives orders for all baby boys in Bethlehem who are two years old or younger to be killed. After Herod's death an angel appears again to Joseph and tells him to return to Israel.

Collect

Almighty God,
who wonderfully created us in your own image
and yet more wonderfully restored us
through your Son Jesus Christ:
grant that, as he came to share in our humanity,
so we may share the life of his divinity;
who is alive and reigns with you,
in the unity of the Holy Spirit,
one God, now and for ever.

Talk/address/ sermon

God's story is a love story that reaches out across the centuries. Its early chapters are recorded in the Old and New Testament, but it continues in our lives today. Today's Old Testament and epistle readings both tell of the constancy of God's love despite the people's unfaithfulness.

Create a time line to show how God has reached out through ordinary people in love. Unroll a large sheet of paper with the following incidents marked on the time line (adding other relevant ones that you might know):

The creation – out of nothing but love God created the world.

God called Abraham into a special covenant relationship.

God called Moses to lead the Israelites into the Promised Land.

The prophets called out to a rebellious people, telling them of God's love and forgiveness.

When the time was right God entered his world to show his love through his son Jesus Christ.

The story goes on through the centuries with God's love being worked out in the lives of ordinary people. We are part of God's love story.

The Isaiah reading points to God's love and care for his people. When they refused to listen to him he was prepared to come into the chaos and evil as a vulnerable baby. Matthew's Gospel shows the vulnerability of Jesus by describing Herod's indiscriminate violent killing of the baby boys. But Jesus wasn't to die as a baby but as an adult, and it was the same violent chaos that led to his death. The reading in Hebrews shows us that it was through his death that we might be saved. God took the risk and joined the mess of humankind out of love.

Prepare two people to come to the front to make a cake. One has a recipe book and is carefully trying to measure ingredients and follow instructions whilst the other won't listen and is not following any instructions. Ask what is likely to be the outcome? God shows us the way to live our lives, but through the centuries people have refused to listen or to follow the instructions. Chaos has been the result: pain, death and pollution etc. are some of the consequences.

Congregational/ group activities

- Divide the congregation into groups and give each group a section of the time line to illustrate, eg.

  group 1 – Creation

  group 2 – Abraham

  Place the time line around the church, leaving an area at the end blank to be used during the prayers.

- In groups, discuss what instructions God has written in the recipe for life. What have been some of the consequences of not following the recipe?

- Jesus' family had to flee from Herod and became refugees. Find out as much information as possible about Christian agencies that work with refugees abroad. Have any of the congregation been refugees? Ask them in advance if they would be prepared to be interviewed in church about their experiences.

Prayers/ intercessions

Let us pray to God our Father because he loves us so dearly.

We pray that the light of the world
may shine so brightly in our lives
that other people notice it
and are attracted to you by the way we live and love.
Pause
Father, live among us; live through our lives.

We pray that the world may stop its noise, chatter and arguing
long enough to hear the angels singing of hope and peace.
Pause
Father, live among us; live through our lives.

Father, we pray for families and all our friends and neighbours;
may every relationship we have be filled with your love.
Pause
Father, live among us; live through our lives

We pray for the homeless and all refugees and exiles;
for all children from broken homes,
and all who are destitute, malnourished or ill.
Pause
Father live among us, live through our lives.

Father we can never thank you enough for coming to rescue us,

and we praise you now and in our lives;
merciful Father
accept these prayers for the sake of your son Jesus Christ. Amen.

> Susan Sayers, 'Christmas 1',
> in *Springboard to Worship* (p. 50)

Stories and other resources

John L. Bell, *He was in the World*, Wild Goose Publications, 1995

'Incarnation', in *Pick and Mix*

Susan Sayers, 'Christmas 1', in *Springboard to Worship*, Kevin Mayhew, 1989

'Red Giant and Red Dwarf', in *50 Five Minute Stories*

'Thanks', in *Best Friends*

Drama

'The Christmas Lecture', in *Sketches from Scripture*

'Arfur's Christmas', in *Playing Up*

Livewires Live (pp. 40 and 41)

 **Music**

Abba, Father, let me be (HON 5, SHF 1)

Adoramus te, Domine (HON 7)

All earth was dark (MP 8)

Angels from the realms of glory (HAMNS 39, HON 34, HTC 77)

Father God I wonder (HON 119, SHF 92)

Love came down at Christmas (HON 320, HTC 62)

See him lying on a bed of straw (HON 440, HTC 91)

The King is among us (HON 483, SHF 511)

Who came to Mary? (BBP 30)

Post communion prayer

Heavenly Father,
whose blessed Son shared at Nazareth
    the life of an earthly home:
help your Church to live as one family,
united in love and obedience,
and bring us all at last to our home in heaven;
through Jesus Christ our Lord.

The Second Sunday of Christmas

 ## Readings

Jeremiah 31.7-14

In earlier chapters Jeremiah has foretold God's judgement on his people and here he describes how God will honour the old covenants and restore and renew the kingdom of Israel (also referred to as Ephraim and Jacob). There will be celebrations by young and old alike, music and dancing, singing and shouting, gladness and joy, with great enjoyment of God's bounty, especially of the food and drink.

Ephesians 1.3-14

Paul attempts throughout this letter to broaden the horizons of the Christians in Ephesus. In this opening section (a single sentence in Greek) he describes what God has done for us in Christ, using dramatic language to emphasize the cosmic and ultimate nature of these actions. Paul emphasizes that we have been chosen, not because we are holy, but in order to become holy, chosen to be God's children, chosen to be part of God's plan.

John1.[1-9]10-18

The great prologue of John's Gospel summarizes the message of the whole book. Jesus who is light and life, came to his rightful place, but was rejected. To those who receive him he brings new birth and divine life as children of God. John pictures the whole cosmos as the setting of that which is being described, reminding us of the beginning in Genesis, and vividly bringing home the reality of the flesh and blood incarnation of Jesus and its significance as grace and truth.

Collect

Almighty God,
in the birth of your Son
you have poured on us the new light of your
     incarnate Word,
and shown us the fullness of your love:
help us to walk in his light and dwell in his love
that we may know the fullness of his joy;
who is alive and reigns with you,
in the unity of the Holy Spirit,
one God, now and for ever.

Talk/address/sermon

One of the strongest associations we make with Christmas is present giving and receiving, an action from one person to another. We also think of the nativity play, a story that happens to individuals. But today's readings make clear that Christmas is more than the sum of the parts of the celebration, the incarnation is a cosmic event which changes the way the world is for everyone. The birth of any child changes the world. Try listing all the effects of your own birth, everything from its effect on world population to the increase in the number of smiles in the house; the birth of Jesus had an added dimension.

 ## Congregational/ group activities

*   'He's got the whole world in his hands' is an appropriate song for today's theme, each group can think up a new verse, complete with actions and/or visual aids. Then the whole song can be learnt and sung at the offertory or other suitable point.

*   Give out candle templates for the groups to cut out their own candles and colour these in. They might wish to write their own prayers on the back of these candles, for use in the prayers/intercessions slot.

*   Make a poster or banner with the words 'Jesus, the light of the world' in the centre. Draw as many kinds of light as possible around the edge (such as a lighthouse, candle, lamps, etc).

 ## Prayers/ intercessions

Use the following intercessions, focusing on us coming before Jesus, the light of the world, in confession:

Jesus, light of the world,
Shine in our darkness.

Lord Jesus Christ, we confess our sins before you.

Forgive us, we pray, for the times we shun your light
and prefer to hide in the darkness of our
hearts . . .
Jesus, light of the world,
Shine in our darkness.

Forgive us, we pray, for the times we do not stand up
for your truth but hide in the darkness . . .
Jesus, light of the world,
Shine in our darkness.

Forgive us, we pray, for our own selfishness and
greed . . .
Jesus, light of the world,
Shine in our darkness.

Forgive us, we pray, for the harmful things we do and
say to others . . .
Jesus, light of the world,
Shine in our darkness.

Forgive us, we pray,
that we live by the light of our own eyes and not by
your light of truth . . .
Jesus, light of the world,
Shine in our darkness.

 ## Stories and other resources

'Jesus is born', in *Livewires Live* (p. 47)

'New babies', in *Under Fives – Alive!*

Donald Dowling, 'Gifts', in *Together through the Bible*, NS/CHP, 1998

 ## Drama

'Christmas with the planimals', in *Playing Up*

'What shall we bring to the baby?', in *Livewires Live*, (pp. 40 and 41)

 ## Music

All over the world (HON 16)

Christ was born in Bethlehem (BBP 36)

God sent his son (WP 58)

Heaven shall not wait (HON 207)

He's got the whole world in his hands (HON 206)

I am a new creation (HON 221, SHF 179)

Infant holy, infant lowly (HON 251, HTC 86)

Once in royal David's city (HAMNS 46, HON 403, HTC 67)

Thou didst leave thy throne (HAMNS 250, HON 513, SHF 552)

Post communion prayer

All praise to you,
almighty God and heavenly King,
who sent your Son into the world
to take our nature upon him
and to be born of a pure virgin:
grant that, as we are born again in him,
so he may continually dwell in us
and reign on earth as he reigns in heaven,
now and for ever.

Epiphany

In any year when there is a Second Sunday of Christmas, the Epiphany may also be celebrated on this Sunday.

The readings are the same in years A, B and C.

 ## *Readings*

Isaiah 60.1-6

These verses from the final section of Isaiah are addressed to those who lived in Judah not long after the return from exile. Into those hard times Isaiah offers the hope of God's future in the picture of a glorious sunrise.

Ephesians 3.1-12

Paul emphasizes that Jesus Christ is for everyone, not just the Jews. This would have been the subject of much debate at the time. Paul makes his position clear, Gentiles have the same inheritance and are part of the same body. The Good News is for everyone.

Matthew 2.1-12

The story of the magi is well known and enjoyed, and has been embellished in many ways down the years. It emphasizes the royal line of Jesus as the magi pay homage and present gifts; it draws attention to the cosmic importance of the event as the stars reveal the birth of Jesus; it encourages us to think of the significance of Jesus for all people as these Gentile astrologers make their long journey.

Collect

> O God,
> who by the leading of a star
> manifested your only Son to the peoples of the
>   earth:
> mercifully grant that we,
> who know you now by faith,
> may at last behold your glory face to face;
> through Jesus Christ your Son our Lord,
> who is alive and reigns with you,
> in the unity of the Holy Spirit,
> one God, now and for ever.

 ## *Talk/address/ sermon*

The star guided the magi throughout their journey. What do you look at to guide you? The answer isn't just God. Christians look to all sorts of people, publications etc., for example, weather forecasts, Radio Times. Show and talk about the things that guide you. Alert some other church members to the question beforehand so that they can contribute. Talk about good reliable guides and bad ones. Talk about trust. Isaiah was heartening the Jews with a vision of the good things that God was going to do – the end of exile. Identify signs of good things around now: locally, nationally and around the world. What hopes do we have for this coming year? How will we realise these hopes and put them into practice? What part will you and I play in the preparation of the kingdom in this new year?

 ## *Congregational/ group activities*

- What presents would you have taken to Bethlehem? Take the group on an imaginary journey. Play relaxing music, encourage relaxation and give a slow gentle outline of the journey with plenty of pauses so that participants have time to imagine all the details. Begin in the warmth of a day in the Middle East, sitting on their front doorstep. Watch passers-by and ask them where they are going. When you hear of the birth, go round the rooms of your house to find a present to take. Walk to the birthplace and present your gift. Remember everything you see, then return home. When everyone is ready, share a little of your journey with one or two others.

- In groups discuss good things. What have you received? What was your favourite present? What did the magi bring? What would you give Jesus? Talk about sharing good things and putting this into practice.

- The magi saw from the stars that Jesus had been born. Cut out stars and write or draw on them things that show that Jesus is born and that God loves us.

- Follow the star! Prepare the sections of the story of the Magi and the Flight to Egypt as readings, dialogues or dramas and present them to the group/congregation in different parts of the worship area, following the star from place to place, perhaps with singing, perhaps collecting symbols or prayers in each place. The new star might be first seen outside or in the porch, Herod's palace will be a splendid part of the church, the birthplace could be the nativity scene, finish with a flight to the quietest corner of the premises.

Prayers/ intercessions

Use the chant 'Kindle a flame to lighten the dark' (*Heaven shall not Wait*, Wild Goose Publications, 1987)

Jesus is a light for the whole world. Borrow or make a large map of the world (the laminated play-mat ones are good) and invite people to place lighted night lights on those places for which they want to pray.

Compose a simple liturgy for a procession of the Magi Crib figures. Turn the manger into a throne. 'Epiphany' means 'manifestation'; make something to take home such as a prayer card or bookmark with an Epiphany design on it – the star, or the three gifts or a CMB: Christe Mansionem Benedica (The piece of chalk activity from *To Dance with God*, Gertrude Mueller Nelson, Paulist Press, 1986)

Use the following response throughout the prayers, or as a blessing at the end of the service:

Leader Christ the light of the world has come:

All **He is the glory of his people –**

Hallelujah! Amen.

Bible Prayers for Worship, 2.8

Stories and other resources

Meryl Doney, *A Lion for the King*, Lion, 1990

Arthur Scholey, *Baboushka*, Lion, 1982

Angela Elwell Hunt, *The Singing Shepherd*, Lion, 1992

Bible Prayers for Worship

 ## Drama

A short drama is included in *Children Aloud!* including a simple song to the tune of 'Three Blind Mice', concluding with an Epiphany question, which could be used in place of a talk.

'The Tune': a short drama or reading for three voices about a boy who visits a baby and a wise man who visits a king . . . (*Wild Goose Prints no.6*, Wild Goose Publications, 1990)

Sue Hardgrave, 'Gifts for the giver', in *Together for Festivals*

 ## Music

All heaven declares (HON 14)

A special star (BBP 37)

As with gladness (HAMNS 51, HON 41, HTC 99)

Be still, for the presence of the Lord (HON 53, SHF 37)

Be thou my vision (HAMNS 343, HON 56, HTC 545, SHF 38)

Come on and celebrate (HON 95, SHF 69)

Keep a light in your eyes for the children of the world (BBP 24)

O worship the Lord in the beauty of holiness (HAMNS 49, HON 394, HTC 344, SHF 429)

Within our darkest night (HON 562)

Post communion prayer

Lord God,
the bright splendour whom the nations seek:
may we who with the wise men
 have been drawn by your light
discern the glory of your presence in your Son,
the Word made flesh, Jesus Christ our Lord.

The Baptism of Christ

The First Sunday of Epiphany

 ## Readings

Isaiah 42.1-9

The first Servant Song emphasizes the importance of exercising fair justice for everyone. It goes on to describe the liberation and the light which is not just for Israel but for all the peoples of the world.

Acts 10.34-43

Peter is talking to friends of Cornelius, having come to the realization that the Good News brought by Jesus Christ (which he summarizes here in eight verses) is for everyone, whatever their nationality.

Matthew 3.13-17

Matthew tells how Jesus came to John the Baptist at the river Jordan to be baptized and saw the Spirit of God descending like a dove. A voice from heaven uses words reminiscent of the Isaiah passage, but describes Jesus as a son rather than a servant.

Collect

Eternal Father,
who at the baptism of Jesus
revealed him to be your Son,
anointing him with the Holy Spirit:
grant to us, who are born again by water and the
    Spirit,
that we may be faithful to our calling
    as your adopted children;
through Jesus Christ your Son our Lord,
who is alive and reigns with you,
in the unity of the Holy Spirit,
one God, now and for ever.

 ## Talk/address/ sermon

Today's collect prays that we 'may be faithful to our calling as your adopted children'. Adopted children are given all the rights of family members. One adopted child was heard to describe the positive aspects of his status in these terms 'my parents chose me, I wasn't just born'. We 'adopt' in other areas, not least cats and dogs and other pets; also foster parents, carers, special people, agencies such as Oxfam, doctors and nurses are all involved in 'adoption'. It is significant that the ministry of Jesus begins with a demonstration and statement of God's love and favour. If we are to be effective and creative we all need to know that we are loved and in receipt of favour.

The task of the disciple of Christ is to engage in the work of delivering God's justice to the whole world. Isaiah and Peter use expansive, demonstrative language to describe the work ahead.

Congregational/ group activities

- The Spirit of God descended on Jesus like a dove, the symbol of Israel or of peace. What would be a good symbol of God's love for you, a sign that God's favour rests on you? You may think about this particularly in terms of your Christian ministry.

- Hands are a good symbol of showing love. Draw round your hand and cut the shape out. Write intercessions on it, or write or draw good, kind things you could do with your hands.

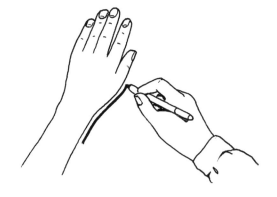

- On a strip of card or paper, write good things you can do. Form the strips into a chain which can be used in Church as an example of a caring community of individuals and as a visual aid for the sermon.

- Symbols and themes are an important part of the Baptism service. Read through parts of the service to identify these. *My Baptism Book* provides a helpful summary to each of these symbols and themes. Draw a picture of the baptism of Christ with a border using these symbols (light and candles, water, cross, etc.).

Prayers/ intercessions

Use part of the service for healing from *The Pattern of our Days*, Wild Goose Publications, 1996 (pp. 64–65). This uses symbols of birth, childhood and adulthood to help us to remember the times that God has helped us throughout our lives.

Alternatively, use the following creed and prayer to focus upon our commitment to Christ:

Let us declare our faith in God:

We believe in God the Father,

From whom every family in heaven and on earth is named.

We believe in God the Son,

Who lives in our hearts through faith,

And fills us with his love.

We believe in God the Holy Spirit,

Who strengthens us with power from on high.

We believe in one God:

Father, Son and Holy Spirit. Amen

Bible Prayers for Worship, 14.13

O Christ the master carpenter, who at the last, through wood and nails, purchased our whole salvation, wield well your tools in the workshop of your world, so that we who come rough-hewn to your bench may here be fashioned to a truer beauty of your hand. We ask it for your own name's sake. **Amen**   (George Macleod)

Stories and other resources

Tim Stafford, *John Porter in Big Trouble*, Lion, 1990

Alan Durant and Chris Riddell, *Angus Rides the Goods Train*, Viking, 1996

Carolyn Nystrom, *Andy's Big Question* (A Child's Guide to Adoption), Lion, 1987

Janet and Allan Ahlberg, *Bye Bye Baby*, Little Mammoth, 1989

Kathleen Crawford, *My Baptism Book*, NS/CHP, 1998

Bible Prayers for Worship

Drama

'Dives' or 'The holy words', in *Act Justly*, Christian Aid/CAFOD, Collins, 1989

Music

Colours of day (HON 87)

Jesus shall take the highest honour (HON 278)

O, let the Son of God enfold you (HON 375, SHF 403)

The Church's one foundation (HAMNS 170, HON 473, HTC 501, SHF 505)

We have a gospel to proclaim (HAMNS 431, HON 532, HTC 519)

When Jesus came to Jordan (HAMNS 526)

Post communion prayer

Lord of all time and eternity,
you opened the heavens
and revealed yourself as Father
in the baptism of Jesus your beloved Son:
by the power of your Spirit
complete the heavenly work of our rebirth
through the waters of the new creation;
through Jesus Christ our Lord.

The Second Sunday of Epiphany

 ## Readings

Isaiah 49.1-7

The second Song of the Servant is spoken by the servant, who is Israel. Israel will be restored and brought back to God and will also become a light to the nations, the means of bringing God's salvation to all parts of the earth.

1 Corinthians 1.1-9

Paul follows his greeting at the beginning of this letter with a passage giving thanks for the members of the church in Corinth and their firm faith. He continually emphasizes their relationship to God through Christ.

John 1.29-42

John the Baptist points out Jesus as the Chosen One of God. When John repeats this the next day, two of his disciples, Andrew and another, begin to follow Jesus instead. Andrew fetches his brother, telling him he has found the Messiah. Simon is given the name Cephas (Peter, the rock) by Jesus.

Collect

Almighty God,
in Christ you make all things new:
transform the poverty of our nature
    by the riches of your grace,
and in the renewal of our lives
make known your heavenly glory;
through Jesus Christ your Son our Lord,
who is alive and reigns with you,
in the unity of the Holy Spirit,
one God, now and for ever.

 ## Talk/address/sermon

Simon is the disciple who will go on to be the leader, the one out in front. But if it hadn't been for quiet Andrew, the one more in the background,

Simon wouldn't have been brought along. Talk about choosing and evaluating how all are different. People who came to Christ were often brought by others. Refer back to last week's theme on doing good things. God's goodness comes through others. Give (and ask for) examples. We need all sorts of people and all need to follow and change and grow in their relationship with God.

Congregational/group activities

- 'We're going on a Bear Hunt' – ask the children or a playgroup leader to teach everyone this classic song/story about discovering and following others on a journey.

- Nicknames – have you got one? Do you know any nicknames for famous people? What nicknames do we give to our friends and why? What nickname would you give yourself and why?

- Play a 'following' game such as 'Follow my Leader' or 'Simon Says', or a trust game.

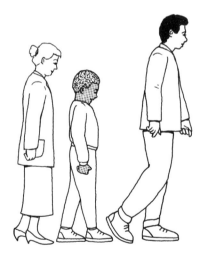

- 'Who am I?' Use blu-tack to stick names of biblical characters onto people's foreheads (ensuring they do not see the name!). They attempt to discover the name of this person, by asking questions from other people (such as 'Am I male or female?', 'Am I in the Old Testament or New Testament?'). They are not allowed to ask the specific question, 'Who am I?' An alternative way to play is to use famous people, movie stars, or names of people who attend church.

Prayers/ intercessions

There are a number of collections of meditations and prayers based specifically on the lectionary. One of the best of these is Edmund Banyard's *Heaven and Charing Cross.* This week's prayer, and the prayers for Epiphany 3 and Proper 2, will use examples from his book.

This week's prayer remembers how Jesus chose not only Simon, but also his quieter brother, Andrew. It was Andrew's readiness to seek out his brother, that led Simon (later called Peter) to meet the Messiah.

Because you found us, Lord,
Because we can share with you
Joys and sorrows,
Fears and hopes;
Because we can share
Every part of our living,
Our days have become that much the richer.
You are both the focus
And the inspiration of our lives.

Remind us,
When we need reminding,
That this richness
Is not for us alone.

Remind us
Of our obligation
To share what we have found
With our sisters and brothers
Whenever
And wherever
We have the opportunity.

'The first thing he did',
in *Heaven and Charing Cross*

Stories and other resources

Janet and Allan Ahlberg, *Bye Bye Baby*, Little Mammoth, 1989

Mike Inkpen, *Threadbear*, Hodder, 1990

Mike Inkpen, *Penguin Small*, Hodder, 1992

Drama

'The Call', in *Eh . . . Jesus . . . Yes, Peter . . .?*, Wild Goose Publications, 1987

 ## Music

God is working his purpose out (HON 172, HTC 191)

God of grace and God of glory (HAMNS 367, HON 174, HTC 324)

James, Andrew, Peter and John (HON 257)

Just as I am, without one plea (HAMNS 246, HON 287, HTC 440)

Keep a light in your eyes (BBP 24)

No one will ever be the same (WGS 2, p. 120)

Post communion prayer

God of glory,
you nourish us with your Word
who is the bread of life:
fill us with your Holy Spirit
that through us the light of your glory
may shine in all the world.
We ask this in the name of Jesus Christ our Lord.

The Third Sunday of Epiphany

Readings

Isaiah 9.1-4

'The people that walked in darkness have seen a great light' – the opening lines bring to mind the great Christmas occasions when the son who is born for us brings the great light. Verse 4 describes the debris of war that will be done away with in the time of peace brought by the new king.

1 Corinthians 1.10-18

Having greeted and affirmed the Christians at Corinth, Paul immediately makes them face up to their problem, namely the factions into which they have formed themselves. It is unthinkable to Paul that Christ's body, the Church, should be divided.

Matthew 4.12-23

Matthew is clear that Jesus is fulfilling many prophecies and here quotes Isaiah. Jesus then calls the first four disciples, Simon (later to be called Peter), Andrew, James and John, who all decide to leave everything in order to follow and learn from Jesus.

Collect

Almighty God,
whose Son revealed in signs and miracles
the wonder of your saving presence:
renew your people with your heavenly grace,
and in all our weakness
sustain us by your mighty power;
through Jesus Christ your Son our Lord,
who is alive and reigns with you,
in the unity of the Holy Spirit,
one God, now and for ever.

Talk/address/sermon

Use nicknames from last week. The twelve were called and became a closely knit band. They must have cared well for each other, to stay together for so long. What makes a 'closely knit band'? Use a visual aid of football fans, uniformed organizations, the family – what are the distinguishing marks of belonging? Changing lifestyle, leaving family, moving away are all stressful activities, the attraction must be real and considerable. What would it take to make you do so? What would the group you were joining need to do to ease the stress for you?

The church at Corinth was beginning to break into sub-groups, as must happen in any organization, but there was clearly antagonism and competitiveness developing too. We often feel a need to reassure ourselves that our views, our sub-group, our attitudes, our music, our theology, or our leaders are better than others, but to engage in such competition is to deny that we are all part of one body. We can be reassured by the love and favour God shows to us in our baptism into the Body.

Congregational/group activities

- The 'great light in the darkness' can be portrayed in many art and craft techniques. Collect different sized jam jars (clear glass is best). Use specialist glass paint to decorate these jars with colourful patterns. Put a 'night light' or small candle inside the jar.

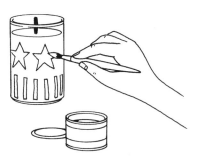

- Try a number of group activity games such as with a large ball, or a parachute. There are a number of books that give suggestions for suitable co-operative games. See the Stories and Other Resources list below for some suggestions. (If you've never tried such games in church, do have a go. Borrow a parachute from your diocesan resource centre.)

- Give everyone a piece of paper the same size. Draw on it something which identifies you (whether this is to do with your role as a parent/child, school/work, hobbies and interests or church life). Make them all into a 'quilt' for the church.

Prayers/ intercessions

The second of the prayers from *Heaven and Charing Cross* uses the passage from Isaiah to meditate on how Jesus' light can gradually reveal both our need for forgiveness and the joys, hopes and new life that Christ brings.

Light a series of candles at the front of the church. Ask the congregation to gather around these as you lead them in the following prayer:

Until the light came,
I did not realize
That I had become so accustomed
To existing in the darkness.

Until the light came,
I did not realize
How much rubbish
I had accumulated about me.

Until the light came,
I did not realize
How small the dwelling
In which I had confined myself.

At first it was dazzling, penetrating,
It wasn't easy to adjust to the light.
Too many things stood revealed
I'd rather not have seen.
Yet gradually,
And with fresh and startling clarity,
New hopes, new joys, new life
Stood revealed,
Waiting for me to grasp them –
If I would!

But I did not have to face
Such decisions –
Until the light came.

Source of light
And source of truth,
Do not allow me
To shut out the light
Which flows from you.
Enable me to face the truth
About myself
Which that light reveals
And strengthens my will

To step with confidence
Into whatever new ways
May open before me.

'The coming of light', in *Heaven and Charing Cross*

Stories and other resources

Michael Foreman, *War and Peas*, Picture Puffin, 1978

David McKee, *Tusk Tusk*, Arrow Books, 1983

Mildred Masheder, *Let's Co-operate (Peaceful Games and Activities)*, Peace Education Project, 1986

Meynell, *Parachute Games*, Meynell Games Publications, 1993

Lesley and Neil Pinchbeck, *Theme Games*, Scripture Union, 1993

Drama

Edmund Banyard, 'The Church that Jack Built', in *Fistful of Fivers*, NCEC, 1986

 # Music

A new commandment (HON 4)

Forth in the peace of Christ we go (HAMNS 458, HON 142, HTC 542)

Jesus calls us o'er the tumult (HAMNS 312, HON 266, HTC 104)

Jesus, hope of every nation (HTC 58)

Jesus we are here (WP 38)

O Lord, all the world belongs to you (HON 378)

What a mighty God we serve (WP 80)

Post communion prayer

Almighty Father,
whose Son our Saviour Jesus Christ
    is the light of the world:
may your people,
illumined by your word and sacraments,
shine with the radiance of his glory,
that he may be known, worshipped, and obeyed
    to the ends of the earth;
for he is alive and reigns, now and for ever.

The Fourth Sunday of Epiphany

 ## Readings

1 Kings 17.8-16

A miraculous story about Elijah. The widow is happy to respond to a normal request for water, but asking for bread is more unexpected and she cannot supply it. Elijah asks her to trust God's promise that her flour and oil will not run out.

1 Corinthians 1.18-31

The world failed to recognize God by using its wisdom. Instead God has made himself known to the 'foolish' through their faith. Asking for signs and endeavouring to become wise will not help in understanding God, but the crucified Christ will. The converts in Corinth were not, in the main, wise and powerful people.

John 2.1-11

The wedding at Cana. This attractive story is a sign giving clues about the whole of Jesus' ministry. Here Jewish legalism, represented by the water pots, becomes the Gospel, the wine which brings gladness to the marriage feast of the kingdom of God. We see the independence of Jesus, acting when the hour comes.

Collect

God our creator,
who in the beginning
commanded the light to shine out of darkness:
we pray that the light of the glorious gospel of Christ
may dispel the darkness of ignorance and unbelief,
shine into the hearts of all your people,
and reveal the knowledge of your glory
  in the face of Jesus Christ your Son our Lord,
who is alive and reigns with you,
in the unity of the Holy Spirit,
one God, now and for ever.

 ## Talk/address/ sermon

Refer to last week and the signs of a community, using the quilt as a visual aid. Talk about the importance of identity in the group. Identify your church's type of community as listed in *Unfinished Business* (CCBI, 1995). Look for signs of the kingdom.

Sharing a celebration is important in the lives of friends, families and communities. We have all built up a picture of Jesus, our pictures will vary, but few of us imagine him as a plump man who likes going to parties. It is clear however that he spent much time eating, drinking, telling stories and engaging in conversation. Celebrating isn't just a matter of having a good time, it makes demands on us – to share ourselves with others, to spend time and money on doing so, to value and listen to people and their stories. We must not keep it to ourselves. We celebrate to enable support through bad times, but we must allow others to access it – this is a primary tool of evangelism.

Congregational/ group activities

- Have a party to celebrate the good things you enjoy, especially ones you may be giving up for Lent: some bread and water to remind you of Elijah, and some water and wine/grape juice to remind you of Cana. The Church celebrates with Holy Communion. Do some of the Talkabout/Take home sheets from *Children and Holy Communion*.

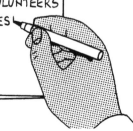

THINGS TO DO

1 MAKE INVITATIONS
2 POST INVITATIONS
3 ORDER DRINKS
4 ARRANGE FOOD
5 ASK FOR VOLUNTEERS
6 CHECK GUES

- Organize a party for a specific occasion (such as Shrove Tuesday). Identify the jobs that need to be done. Invitations need to be made and sent, food and drink arranged and a guest list drawn up. Who should be invited? This links with the talk session about access and evangelism.

- In groups, discuss different things that we can thank God for – whether these have happened in people's own lives, or in the life of the church or nation, or were world events. Draw pictures of these, or write thank-you prayers on small pieces of paper. Blow up large balloons and, very carefully, sellotape these prayers or drawings to the balloons.

- Study in groups the different models of church life in *Unfinished Business*.

Prayers/ intercessions

Ask several children to collect in the balloons with the different thank-you prayers on them. Use the prayers on these balloons alongside the following prayers:

Father in Heaven, we thank you for all the times
We can celebrate and remember.
Help us to remember truthfully and celebrate joyfully
All the good things you have done for us.
Amen

Thank you, Lord, for all the memories you give me –
For people who mean so much to me: friends, relatives,
And people I meet along the way;
For happy times and sad times,
Exciting times and times when there was not much to interest me.
Help me to use my precious memories
To be a better follower of you.
Amen

Children Celebrate! (p. 3)

 ## Stories and other resources

Rachel Hall and Arthur Baker, *Jesus Goes to a Wedding*, Kevin Mayhew, 1993

Nick Butterworth and Mike Inkpen, *The Cat's Tale*, Collins Picture Lion, 1988

David McKee, *Elmer*, Andersen, 1989

Unfinished Business

Children Celebrate! (pp. 1–3)

 ## Music

Adoramus te, Domine (HON 7)

All my hope on God is founded (HAMNS 336, HON 15, HTC 451)

Immortal, invisible, God only wise (HAMNS 199, HON 242, HTC 21, SHF 210)

Inspired by love and anger (HON 252)

Laudate Dominum (HON 291)

Lift high the cross! (HAMNS 72, HON 303, HTC 508)

Purify my heart (HON 428)

Post communion prayer

Generous Lord,
in word and eucharist we have proclaimed
the mystery of your love:
help us so to live out our days
that we may be signs of your wonders in the world;
through Jesus Christ our Saviour.

The Presentation of Christ in the Temple

Candlemas (2 February)

Candlemas is celebrated either on 2 February or on the Sunday falling between 28 January and 3 February

 ## Readings

The principal service readings are the same for Years A, B and C. These are:

Malachi 3.1-5: The coming of the Lord brings a time of purification

Hebrews 2.14-18: Because Christ suffered when he was tempted, he can help all those who suffer temptations

Luke 2.22-40: The presentation of Jesus at the temple

The alternative readings, for the Second Service, are described below in full.

Haggai 2.1-9

The prophet brings God's promise, established in the Covenant and still alive through the Spirit (v.5). They have not been forgotten. Part of the call to the Remnant of Israel is to rebuild the Temple, but the promise also looks forward to Jesus –'the desired of all nations' (v.7). There is a lovely image here of Christ's presentation in the Temple confirming the promise in v.9 – 'in this place I will bring peace . . . here the Prince of Peace'. The promise is fulfilled in both parts.

John 2.18-22

This passage gives us the direct link between the Temple building and the person of Jesus. One is the symbol of God's presence among His people; the other is Immanuel, 'God with us'. The people demand a sign, a proof of who Jesus is . . . and they take Jesus' words literally (well, who wouldn't !). The explanation (v.22) simply underlines the 'new thing' Haggai declares – God has bigger plans than we can imagine!

Collect

Almighty and ever-living God,
    clothed in majesty,
whose beloved Son
    was this day presented in the Temple,
in substance of our flesh:
grant that we may be presented to you
with pure and clean hearts,
by your Son Jesus Christ our Lord,
who is alive and reigns with you,
in the unity of the Holy Spirit,
one God, now and for ever.

 ## Talk/address/sermon

Being forgotten: how does it feel to be forgotten – to be waiting for someone, unsure if they are going to turn up? Imagine how the people of Israel must have felt, in exile, waiting for God . . . and see how God's promise is such a wonderful answer to their cries.

Limiting God: how do we limit God? Have a big cardboard box – tell the congregation that God is inside . . . that if we ask Him, He will come out like a genie. This may initially appear offensive, but use this to teach that this is how we often treat God. We pray as if He will grant our wishes, and get cross when things don't happen as we would want! People did not expect Jesus – He was not what they wanted – yet He was the key to God's plan of salvation, and still is.

 ## Congregational/group activities

- Make a large card. On the front cover, draw the shape of a temple/church with a window in it. On the inside facing page write the name 'JESUS' in large letters. The overall effect is that in looking

through the window, we see Jesus, bigger than our window, to illustrate that our view of him is often small and constraining.

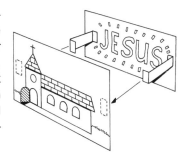

- This needs to be set up beforehand. Arrange to have 4 people, holding hands, to surround whoever is leading or speaking in the service. Whenever someone gets up to speak, read, lead, they are surrounded and contained. This is both fun, and disruptive, but it serves to show how limiting it is to be 'contained'– yet we often try to contain God!

- Escapologist: it would be great to use a trained escapalogist, who can be trussed up in a straitjacket and then escape (British Youth For Christ often have people on their lists) – it is a wonderfully dynamic illustration of breaking out of limitations.

- Use the box idea in the second talk. Put a slot in the top, and get people to write prayer requests on pieces of paper, and then post them into the box – like a ballot box. Have a short script of children asking what the people are doing, and have another child explain that they are putting prayers into the box, because *that's where God is*. It is a silly idea, yet a simple illustration.

- Christingle: some churches hold their Christingle Service at Candlemas instead of before Christmas. The candle in the orange is the symbol of Christ's presence in the world.

Prayers/ intercessions

Use the following suggestion, adapted from Judith Merrell's book *One hundred and one Ideas for Creative Prayers*.

In the group activities, ask people to list the times when it is good to know that we can trust God to be with us and to help us. Use these suggestions as part of the following responsive prayer:

Thank you, Father, that when we are nervous or afraid . . .
We can trust in you.
Thank you that when we have a difficult decision to make . . .
We can trust in you.
Thank you that when we are in an awkward situation . . .
We can trust in you.
Thank you that when we are in trouble . . .
We can trust in you.

Thank you that when there is no one else to turn to . . .
We can trust in you.
Thank you that whatever we are doing, when we need help . . .
We can trust in you.
Thank you, Lord, that we can depend on you, because you never let anyone down.
Amen

'Trusting in God', in *One Hundred and One Ideas for Creative Prayers* (No. 37)

Stories and other resources

Show a video clip from *Free Willy* – the last scene where the whale is captured in the harbour, and breaks free by jumping the harbour wall. This is an example of breaking out of restrictions, and can fit into the theme of God breaking out of the restrictions we put round Him.

'Candlemas service and talk', in *Children Aloud!*

Elizabeth Speight, 'Celebrating Candlemas', in *Together for Festivals*

Judith Merrell, *One hundred and One Ideas for Creative Prayers*, Scripture Union, 1995

 ## Music

All earth was dark (MP 8)

Christ whose glory fills the skies (HAMNS 4, HON 82, HTC 266)

Hail to the Lord who comes (HAMNS 314)

Jesus bids us shine (JP 128)

Laudate Dominum (HON 291)

Love divine, all loves excelling (HAMNS 131, HON 321, HTC 217, SHF 353)

My Jesus, my saviour (SH 94)

The light of Christ has come into the world (MP 652)

Post communion prayer

Lord, you fulfilled the hope of Simeon and Anna,
who lived to welcome the Messiah:
may we, who have received these gifts beyond words,
prepare to meet Christ Jesus when he comes
to bring us to eternal life;
for he is alive and reigns, now and for ever.

Sunday between 3 and 9 February

(if earlier than the Second Sunday before Lent)

Proper 1

Readings

Isaiah 58.1-9a[b-12]

Here is a reflection on true fasting – not a religious show, to tell everyone how pious we are, but a dedication of our lives. The people are in rebellion against God, and yet expect Him to be impressed by their fasting. God sees through the sham, and calls them to a true fast, reflected in their behaviour.

1 Corinthians 2.1-12 [13-16]

What is our faith based on? Paul tells us of his presentation of Christ crucified (v.2) and the Spirit's power (v.4) – a message not of human wisdom, but of God. For it is only by the Spirit that God reveals His mind. This means our faith is dependent upon Him, not on our own resources, intellect, or reckoning.

Matthew 5.13-20

Salt and Light: two opposites, yet Jesus uses these elements to teach us about our work in the world. Salt, hidden, preserving, changing from within, and light, only useful when visible, shining from the outside. Jesus tells us we are neither salt or light – but both.

Talk/address/ sermon

Fasting: how is our faith shown in action? What part should fasting play? Like unseen preparations for a meal, or a party, the results are seen in the event. So it is with fasting. It is an unseen preparation for our daily lives as Christians, trusting ourselves to God. As Jesus said, what is in our hearts is seen in our actions.

Salt and Light: this talk needs visual aids: a lamp, two bowls of food, one salted, the other not. Use them to explain the differences between salt and light, and make a chart, or OHP slide itemizing them. Then remind people that Jesus tells us to be BOTH. How do we do that in our daily lives? This can be explored in a group activity (see below).

Big-head: it is so easy to think we know best – and end up ignoring God. We can be blinded by clever arguments, sophistication, attractive sin. We can make our own decisions based on what we feel like, and ignore God.

Congregational/ group activities

- Have two large signs 'Salt' and 'Light' and ask the congregation to split into two groups – according to the one they prefer. Each group is to explore how they can be that element (i.e. the salt group explore how they can be salt). Make a list of these things. Then at another point in the service, get each group to explore how they can be the other element (i.e. the 'salt' group explore how they can be 'light'). Use each list of things to show how we are called to be both. Is the Church both, or are we as individuals both?

- Make a list of all the things we need to 'dedicate' to God. These may be things or people we need to offer to God and they can be brought up to the Communion Table as part of our offering. It is so easy for God to be squeezed out of our faith, and for other things get in the way of Him. This is one way of regaining the right perspective of trust in our faith.

- Use a liturgical response to prepare for Communion, or as a dedication in the service. This can be written by groups during the service itself as a group activity, or prepared beforehand. There is an example in the 'Prayer' section below.

Prayers/intercessions

Gather the children together and, over a table or bowl, pour salt into their hands. Pray for our witness as 'salt' in our community: this will include our school. Then light some candles and get some of the children to hold them (children are usually very careful, but have one or two adults there to make sure!). Pray about our witness as light in our community.

A liturgical suggestion before Communion:

Lord you called us salt, but we are not very good at
   using the gifts You've given us to flavour the world.
Lord forgive us and make us new
Lord You called us light, but we have not kept the light
   You entrusted to us burning brightly.
Lord forgive us and make us new
Jesus said 'You are the salt of the earth . . . You are
   the light of the world'
Lord restore our vision of You;
make us faithful as You are faithful,
so that when You come in glory
we may hear You say,
'Welcome into the joy of the Lord.'
Amen

Stories and other resources

Video clip – something from a 'Wind in the Willows' episode showing Mr Toad being conceited and big-headed, and yet then getting it all wrong!

David Adam, *Border Lands*, SPCK, 1991 (p. 81 – A lovely prayer of dedication)

There are also sections on 'Commitment' in the *Iona Community Worship Book* (pp. 44–5/83–6)

Leslie Francis and Nicola Slee, *Teddy Horsley: A Grumpy Day*, NCEC, 1994

'God's Call', in *Jigsaw*, Crusaders, 1995

Drama

'Careless Talk', in *A Fistful of Sketches*

Music

Abba Father (HON 5, MP 3, SHF 1)

Blest are the pure in heart (HAMNS 238, HON 63, HTC 110, SHF 40)

Father I place into Your hands (HON 121, SHF 94)

Glory be to Jesus (HAMNS 66, HON 159, HTC 126, SHF 125)

Holy, holy, holy, Lord God almighty (HAMNS 95, HON 212, SHF 168)

I, the Lord of sea and sky (HON 235)

It's an adventure (JP 399)

I will offer up my life (SH 65)

Lord, make me a mountain (MP 436)

The Summons (Will you come and follow me?) (HON 560)

Thy kingdom come, O God (HAMNS 177, HON 519, HTC 334)

Collect and post communion prayer

Advent 1998 to Advent 1999	**The Proper 1 service**
Advent 2001 to Advent 2002	**material is not**
Advent 2004 to Advent 2005	**required for these years**

Sunday between 10 and 16 February

(if earlier than the Second Sunday before Lent)

Proper 2

 ### Readings

Deuteronomy 30.15-20

Here's a challenge. To love leads to life; to reject love leads to destruction. God gives an ultimatum – an offer of life . . . or death. It is in terms of a command, so that the choice is about obedience. This was always a key aspect of the Old Testament relationship between God and his people.

or

Ecclesiasticus 15.15-20

The wisdom of the Lord is extolled. He sees everything and notes every human action.

1 Corinthians 3.1-9

Divided loyalties in the church . . . different camps, personalities, and Paul's answer. How futile it all is when people are simply fulfilling their calling in different ways. This is how the church grows, yet we do so like to divide into groups.

Matthew 5.21-37

Jesus explores aspects of the Old Testament Law, and digs deeper – revealing the spirit of the Law behind the mere words. The Law is about a pure heart, not so much about controlled actions.

Talk/address/ sermon

Making choices: we make some choices where a lot is at stake. How do we decide? There seems to be no bigger choice than the one that faced the people of Israel that day. What would you have decided, and why?

Divided loyalties: we are used to separating over supporting football teams, and such like. How foolish to be divided over the same team! At our local team ground, there was an end of loyal supporters called the 'Moaners' End' – because there were always critical noises coming from that end! It was not much good for the team! How does this relate to the church?

The Law: Jesus' explanation of these commands shows that God is more concerned about the heart than the final action. This does not mean that our actions are unimportant, but that it is more important for the heart to be right. Why do you think that is?

 ### Congregational/ group activities

- Identical packages: wrap up 5 identical packages, with different things in, but one contains a valuable prize. Ask someone to choose which one contains the prize. Why is this so difficult? It's because they all look the same, and we can't see inside. If you are brave, you could then ask 5 adults to stand at the front and ask the same person which is the most valuable . . . and why?

- Divided we fall: split the church into three groups (men/women/children) and give three volunteers a task each (e.g. change a light bulb on a table lamp; open a carton of milk and pour it into a glass; put together a 6–8 piece child's jigsaw). Then blindfold them! The 3 'teams' then shout out instructions – but they can only shout out one thing (e.g. 'Pull the lever!'). The result is a lot of noise, and instructions shouted at the wrong time etc. . . . and the task does not get done very easily. We each have different tasks in the church – the best way is to encourage and help each other instead of competing against each other.

- Try writing a sketch along the lines of three distinct people groups e.g.:

A 'I look down on him/her because I read *The Times.*'

B 'I look up to him because he reads *The Times* and I only read the *Mail.*'

C 'I can't read yet!'

A   'I look down on him because I know my Bible well.'

B   'I look up to him because I can never find the right passage in time!'

C   'I saw myself in one of those Bible stories last week.'

Prayers/ intercessions

Use the following prayer from *Heaven and Charing Cross* to reflect upon our own struggles with difficult decisions and between good and evil. It is based upon the Deuteronomy reading for today.

'Today I offer you the choice of life and good, or death and evil.'

Deuteronomy 30.15 REB

For me,
It's seldom as simple as that.
Choices are blurred,
One thing has to be weighed
With another,
All too often
There is no obvious clear-cut good,
But only the choice
Between varying degrees
Of evil.
Not black or white,
But only indeterminate
Shades of grey.

This I pray, my Lord,
To you, who know my weaknesses.
When I am confused,
The way ahead is far from clear
And I must make difficult choices;
Though I may not see
The distant goal,
Grant me
Guidance for each next step
As it must be taken,
That I stray not over-far
From the path to life.
Amen.

'Choices', in *Heaven and Charing Cross*

There is also a prayer of commitment in *Project Joshua* (CPAS, 1997, p. 35). This is a good way of making a choice of commitment in a responsive way from the text of Joshua 24.

John 17 – Jesus prays for us to be united. This passage could form the basis of your own praying – and could be explored in groups, and then the prayers used in the service.

Stories and other resources

One Hundred and One Ideas for Creative Prayers (no.12) 'The Church' – a good way of recognizing our different groups and needs, and even opinions, yet we are all together in the one place/church/faith.

'Families', in *Children Aloud!* (p. 46)

'Fellow Travellers', in *All Aboard!*

'Choices', in *Pick and Mix* (p. 31)

Obsession (by the music group Delirious?) – 'My heart burns for you' (on *Cutting Edge* vol. 4)

Drama

Dave Hopwood, 'The case of the golden calf', in *Playing Up*

Music

A new commandment (HON 4, SHF 14)

Create in me a clean heart O God (MP 108)

Forgive our sins as we forgive (HAMNS 362, HON 141, HTC 111)

For I'm building a people of power (HON 135, SHF 109)

Jesus put this song into our hearts (HON 275, MP 376)

Lord, you have my heart (SH 87)

Purify my heart (HON 428)

Take my life and let it be (HAMNS 249, HON 464, HTC 554, SHF 496)

The Church's one foundation (HAMNS 170, HON 473, HTC 501, SHF 505)

Collect and post communion prayer

Advent 1998 to Advent 1999	The Proper 2 service
Advent 2001 to Advent 2002	material is not
Advent 2004 to Advent 2005	required for these years

Sunday between 17 and 23 February

(if earlier than the Second Sunday before Lent)

Proper 3

 ### Readings

Leviticus 19.1-2,9-18

'Be holy because I, the Lord your God, am holy.' This is a passage which enlarges on this declaration by God to the people of Israel. Although these are simple commands that underline the ten commandments, they are punctuated by a reminder 'I am the Lord'. It is like a chorus, so that as this part of the Law was read aloud, so the people joined in with the refrain. It's a good way of reading it today, as it encourages us to reflect on the Lord.

1 Corinthians 3.10-11,16-23

As the Old Testament passage reminds us that the Law is God's initiative, so Paul tells this New Testament church the same thing. Jesus is their foundation for faith and there is no other. The building above that foundation is for worship, as the Holy Spirit dwells in our hearts – a sacred, living temple (v.16/17). Therefore there is no reason to boast about who helped lay that foundation (whether Paul or Apollos or Peter . . .). The important thing is that the building is God's – foundation, structure and contents!

Matthew 5.38-48

This passage in the Sermon on the Mount deals with those people we would not call friends – but the opposite! A system of taking revenge and retribution has no place in God's kingdom. As in previous weeks, Jesus goes below the letter of the Old Testament Law, and turns it upside down. Here, rather than take revenge, try love and forgiveness instead. Love for one's enemies shows God's love. This is the love He shows for us in sending Jesus in the first place, and He calls us to exercise that same quality of love for each other.

Talk/address/sermon

The Temple of the Holy Spirit: what does this mean? The Spirit dwells in us (as Jesus promised in John 14.17). How does this affect our lives, worship, attitudes and character? What does it mean when linked with that statement from Leviticus 'Be holy because I, the Lord your God, am holy'? We can be holy only because the Holy Spirit dwells within us.

Love for enemies: why is it so hard for us to love our enemies? It is much easier to want to take revenge. Humanly it is so difficult to love our enemies. It is God's spirit dwelling in us that enables us to forgive – it is the Spirit that brings God's love with him, so we can love as God wants with his love.

Congregational/group activities

- *Get Your Own Back* – a VERY popular children's TV programme. Try staging something like it, but watch it first to understand the importance of why the child wants to get their own back on the adult. Then do a kind of quiz – or challenges – even have some 'gunge' at the end . . . encouraging the children to cheer on the child competitor! The noise will be interesting as the adults will (hopefully) join in cheering their 'side' too.

- In groups, make a list of working rules for your church (e.g. always do as the vicar says). Encourage them to say how hard these might be, and to think of exceptions to these rules (e.g. only do what he/she says if you agree with them – otherwise they must  be mad!) This activity may lead you to interesting discoveries about our view of authority and 'law'. It could be quite lively!

- This week's focus on the spirit might give an opportunity for ministry during/after the service – as we recognize the Holy Spirit's place in us to help us love, and enable us to worship. This might raise areas where people need prayer.

- The Trail of Revenge. Set up a ring of people. The first one begins with a grievance

  A   'You pushed me over and I hurt my knee!'

  B   'I only did that because your brother wouldn't lend me a pencil.'

  C   'I didn't lend you my pencil because when I lent her one, she never gave it back.'

  D   'I didn't give it back because he took it off me.'

  E   'I wanted to get back at you because your friend told tales about me to the teacher.'

  F   'I only did that because your friend got me into trouble last week.'

It would be fun to then bring it back to the first one, so it goes round and round.

This is a children's version, but an adult one could be quite interesting – and maybe painful! Perhaps it might be a congregational activity to write one! Perhaps a Jesus figure could break into the circle at some stage and show how the Holy Spirit can break the cycle?

 **Prayers/ intercessions**

Use the following Confession:

Lord God,
For the times when we think we are better than others,
We are sorry.
For the times we have told lies,
We are sorry.
For the times we have joined in with others who are doing wrong,
We are sorry.
For the times we have shouted at our friends and family,
We are sorry.

For the times when we have refused to apologize,
We are sorry.
For the times when we've ganged up against others,
We are sorry.
For the times when we were too busy with our own affairs to notice that other people needed help.
We are sorry.
For these and all other wrongs,
We are sorry.
Amen

'We are sorry', in *One Hundred and One Ideas for Creative Prayers* (No. 26)

 Stories and other resources

Video clip of 'Matilda', showing where she takes revenge on parents, brother, or Miss Trunchbull!

'Jesus teaches about lifestyle', in *Livewires Live* (pp. 40 and 41)

Leslie Francis and Nicola Slee, *Teddy Horsley: A Grumpy Day*, NCEC, 1994

Bob Hartman, *The Lion Storyteller Bedtime Book*, Lion, 1998

Taffy Davis, *Miles and the Computer,* Scripture Union, 1987 (A great story about forgiveness, and introduces the idea that as God forgives us, we need to forgive. This will need extending to enemies!)

 **Music**

Christ is our cornerstone (HAMNS 161, HON 77, HTC 564)

God forgave my sin (HON 167, SHF 126)

I am trusting thee, Lord Jesus (HON 223, HTC 433, SHF 183)

I will build my Church (MP 305)

The Lord is King! Lift up thy voice (HAMNS 107, HON 485, HTC 183, SHF 519)

The wise man built his house upon the rock (JP 252)

You are holy (JP 500)

Collect and post communion prayer

Advent 1998 to Advent 1999	The Proper 3 service
Advent 2001 to Advent 2002	material is not
Advent 2004 to Advent 2005	required for these years

The Second Sunday Before Lent

 ## Readings

Genesis 1.1 - 2.3

The story of Creation. God's great initiative begins, apparently in the only correct scientific order for life to begin and be sustainable. Notice too the change in the method – God sets up the environment, and then (in v.24) we see *the land* producing, rather than 'let there be . . .' The stage is set, and the wheels of life begin to turn. There is also the focus at the end on man, the image of God, and the charge to be stewards over creation.

Romans 8.18-25

The future hope of redeeming creation – fallen after the arrival of disobedience and sin into that first picture of God's perfect, pleasing creation. Paul talks about liberation, waiting and groaning, frustration and decay. The image of pregnancy is quite strong here.

Matthew 6.25-34

Don't worry! How easy it is to focus on everyday concerns – and lose sight of God's Kingdom. There is a lovely link here with the picture of creation and our future hope. We can get so depressed by the state of the world today, but Jesus says 'don't worry – it is in God's hands and plan'.

Collect

> Almighty God,
> you have created the heavens and the earth
> and made us in your own image:
> teach us to discern your hand in all your works
> and your likeness in all your children;
> through Jesus Christ your Son our Lord,
> who with you and the Holy Spirit
>   reigns supreme over all things,
> now and for ever.

 ## Talk/address/ sermon

Creation is spoilt and in need of 'redeeming' – this gives a good opportunity to do a kind of evangelistic talk, taking the theme from these readings. Creation, so good and promising at first, spoilt by sin, but God has a plan to redeem. Then Jesus' command 'Seek first the Kingdom of God . . .' This can be used as a strong call to turn to Him. There is a suggested drama below that would fit in well.

Worries: there are so many things we get in a stew about – what does it mean to trust God with them? What does this promise from Jesus' lips mean in 6.33? You could link this passage with John 14.1 (about trusting in God even when we are afraid – maybe the next stage on from being worried).

 ## Congregational/ group activities

- Creation reading: it would be good to have this read by different readers (you could use 7), with all reading the choral line at the end of each day 'And God saw that it was good'.

- Invite along a potter or painter to create something in the service – and then, having asked their permission beforehand, spoil it. The effect is very powerful, as we see something good and beautiful that is then spoiled wilfully. It's a good visual aid of the spoiling of creation – both initially and now – often wilfully. It can be done just as effectively with 'Duplo' bricks, but ask an adult to build something to avoid tears when it is dropped on the floor and broken!

- Write out some of the things that worry us; another group could find as many verses or passages in the Bible which say 'Do not be afraid/worried'. These could then be matched with the worries – and we should see that the promises/reassurances far outweigh the worries.

Prayers/ intercessions

What are you worried about? Make a list of 'worries' on an OHP acetate in washable pen, and then write out Matthew 6.33 over them in a permanent pen. As we offer these things to God in prayer, *very carefully* wipe across the acetate with a damp cloth; the worries disappear and the verse is left.

Prepare a time of repentance – especially as we lead up to Lent – for the way we have not been good stewards of creation.

Stories and other resources

There is a useful selection of prayers, songs and liturgies in *Rhythm of Life* by David Adam (SPCK, 1996), Section 2 'Creation', and also in *The Iona Community Worship Book* (pp. 40–1 and 79–82)

'God as creator', in *Jigsaw*, Crusaders, 1995

Carine Mackenzie, *The Caring Creator*, Christian Focus, 1992

Rick Mundschuh and Tom Finley, *Kick Starters*, Zondervan, 1996

Drama

'In the beginning', in *Acting Up*

Music

All creatures of our God and King (HAMNS 105, HON 9, HTC 13)

All things bright and beautiful (HAMNS 116, HON 21)

Do not be worried and upset (MP 117)

Father God I wonder (HON 119, MP 128, SHF 92)

God is great (TS 126)

I'm special (MP 325)

My God is so big (JP 169)

Seek ye first (HON 442)

Thou whose almighty word (HAMNS 180, HON 514, HTC, 506, SHF 554)

You're my maker (JP 503)

Post communion prayer

God our creator,
by your gift
the tree of life was set at the heart of the earthly paradise,
and the bread of life at the heart of your Church:
may we who have been nourished at your table on earth
be transformed by the glory of the Saviour's cross
and enjoy the delights of eternity;
through Jesus Christ our Lord.

The Sunday Next Before Lent

 ## Readings

Exodus 24.12-18

The confirming of the Covenant – Moses and Joshua go up the mountain into God's presence. The cloud (and fire) that had been part of the leading of the people out of Egypt cover the mountain to signify God's presence. As Moses enters God's presence, and stays there 40 days, there is a physical representation of the Covenant – a relationship between God and man. This relationship is made on God's terms, not ours.

2 Peter 1.16-21

Peter reflects on his experience on the mount of Transfiguration (the Gospel reading) and again Peter underlines God's initiative in this and in the revelation of prophecy. It is important to Peter's testimony that he was 'an eyewitness' to this event, and that he recognized the glory given to Jesus. 'Glory' is one of the words that the Bible uses to signify God's presence.

Matthew 17.1-9

The Transfiguration – Jesus, the Law, and the Prophets, and God's declaration are all included here, as at Jesus' baptism – only this time with 'Listen to Him' added. This underlines Jesus' own statement that He has come to fulfil the Law and the Prophets (Matthew 5.17). Here He is seen to be greater, to have a stronger 'voice' than them. He is the One through whom we now have our relationship with God as Father.

Collect

Almighty Father,
whose Son was revealed in majesty
before he suffered death upon the cross:
give us grace to perceive his glory,
that we may be strengthened to suffer with him
and be changed into his likeness, from glory to
    glory;
who is alive and reigns with you,
in the unity of the Holy Spirit,
one God, now and for ever.

 ## Talk/address/ sermon

A simple exposition of the place of Jesus as the glorified Son of God. What place does He have in our lives?

Coming to God – the importance of being in God's presence. This can be a good preparation for Lent, exploring how we can come into God's presence today, and stay there with Him. This is a time for developing our relationship with Him, of discovering His love for us, as we obediently come to Him. This can sound very abstract . . . so it needs to be combined with a congregational activity (below).

 ## Congregational/ group activities

- Coming to God: in groups, share together about things that have helped you discover God's love and places you go to meet Him. This will show how we are all different in our meeting with God, and that can be very helpful. It may also encourage each other to discover more about God.

- Tent of Meeting: this was one way the people of Israel met God – Moses and Joshua went to a tent set up outside the camp. As a symbol of God's presence, it could be quite fun to build one in church and have this up during Lent. There is a pattern in *Project Joshua* (CPAS, 1997).

- Banner of Glory: use lots of silver and gold paper/material to reflect the sunlight – the effect is stunning. Use this to talk about our witness and how we reflect the glory of God as lights in the world.

Prayers/intercessions

Explore God's presence, either using some of the places raised in the activity time or, even better, with OHP photographs or pictures of places. These need to be prepared beforehand.

Rhythm of Life by David Adam (p. 26) gives a good opening responsive prayer about God's presence, glory, and creation.

Use the following prayers to prepare the congregation for Lent. The theme of the prayers is 'Ready to serve God'.

Jesus came among us not to give orders, but to be a servant.
Following this example, we pray . . .
Make us ready to serve you, Lord.

Our world needs to hear about Jesus as urgently now as then. We pray . . .
Make us ready to serve you, Lord.

Still Jesus needs people to bring love and peace between parents and children. We pray . . .
Make us ready to serve you, Lord.

Still Jesus needs people to turn the disobedient back to God's way. We pray . . .
Make us ready to serve you, Lord.

Jesus is coming again soon. Looking forward to that day, we pray . . .
Make us ready to serve you, Lord.

A Church for All Ages (p. 155)

Stories and other resources

Project Joshua, CPAS, 1997

David Adam, *Rhythm of Life*, SPCK, 1996

Leslie Francis and Nicola Slee, *Teddy Horsley: Good Morning*, NCEC, 1994

'Names are special', in *Best Friends*

'Family', in *Children Aloud!* (pp. 46–49)

More Things to Do in Children's Worship

 ## Music

By your side (SH 16)

Christ is the world's true light (HAMNS 346, HON 78, HTC 323)

Christ whose glory fills the skies (HAMNS 4, HON 82, HTC 266)

Come and see (HON 88)

Come, praise the name of Jesus (HTC 538)

Draw near to God (MP 118)

Glory, glory in the highest (MP 174)

God is working His purpose out (MP189)

My lips shall praise you (SH 95, TS 369)

To be in your presence (SH 135, TS 524)

Post communion prayer

Holy God,
we see your glory in the face of Jesus Christ:
may we who are partakers at his table
reflect his life in word and deed,
that all the world may know
his power to change and save.
This we ask through Jesus Christ our Lord.

The First Sunday of Lent

 ## Readings

Genesis 2.15-17; 3.1-7

God places the first created man in the garden of Eden, to look after it. The man has complete freedom to eat anything, except from the tree of the knowledge of good and evil. Then the serpent comes and persuades the first created woman to eat from the forbidden tree, so that she might gain knowledge and wisdom. She shares the fruit with the man, who willingly takes it. Suddenly they are aware of their nakedness and they cover themselves.

Romans 5.12-19

Paul regards death as the punishment meted out by God to humankind, for Adam's sin in eating from the tree of the knowledge of good and evil. He points out that just as one man brought so much sin and death, so another – Jesus – brought the great and wonderful gift of grace and justification from God.

Matthew 4.1-11

This is an account of Jesus fasting for 40 days, and enduring great waves of temptation during that time. In extreme hunger he is tempted to change stones into bread; in a great yearning for change in people's hearts he is tempted to gain absolute power; in a struggle with the conviction of his identity he is tempted to test God's love and purpose for him.

Collect

Almighty God,
whose Son Jesus Christ fasted forty days in the
   wilderness,
and was tempted as we are, yet without sin:
give us grace to discipline ourselves
   in obedience to your Spirit;
and, as you know our weakness,
so may we know your power to save;
through Jesus Christ your Son our Lord,
who is alive and reigns with you,
in the unity of the Holy Spirit,
one God, now and for ever.

 ## Talk/address/ sermon

Why is knowledge of good and evil so dangerous for human beings? Perhaps it is because we get too big for our boots; and that is probably because we seek confidence in the wrong things! If only we could simply trust in God's love and see ourselves in the context of a bigger picture. Humankind needs to remember God's deity, and our place within the created order as stewards of the earth.

The Romans reading shows the amazing and limitless love of God, which goes on being shown to us, despite our resistance to it. Free gifts are always given for a reason: perhaps to win us over? What is God's reason for giving us the free gift of his love?

The Matthew reading is a striking insight into Jesus' humanity as he struggles with the reality of people's resistance to God's love. At the same time, Jesus' response to each temptation focuses entirely on the will of God, as though that is where every ounce of his being is founded.

 ## Congregational/ group activities

- In groups write up to ten tasks as a job description for God's Earth Steward. Which two would God think were the most important? Share your top two with the other groups.

- Using newspaper cuttings, make a collage of the good and evil in the world.

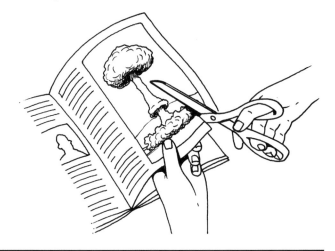

- In the Gospel reading, Jesus was tempted to gain absolute power. Ask whether it would be preferable if God was a magician and could simply wave a wand to feed the hungry, heal the sick, make bad people good and sad people happy. Ensure that the answers are listened to carefully – perhaps write some views down to offer in prayer later on.

- Dramatize the temptations and then, with Matthew in mind, ask everyone to form WCCs i.e. World Changing Committees! They have limitless power and have to decide what changes they would make and how such changes would be implemented. Having listed the changes and the plans of how to carry them out, ask if God would agree with the plans? Where would the differences lie? Are there any links with the way Jesus was tempted to change things in the Matthew account?

- On a piece of paper, write or draw something which you want to offer in praise, supplication, thanksgiving, intercession, etc. to God's generous love. Then make a huddled circle with several willing members of the congregation, holding hands. Have a child shout out, 'How big is God's love?' The circle stretches a bit, becoming bigger and the people reply 'This big!' Repeat the question and answer until the circle is stretched to breaking point, even collapsing.

Prayers/ intercessions

With God's love circle, from Activity 5, at its most stretched, scatter within it the pieces of paper. Give thanks that God's love is bigger than all the love in this church and even the world, and God's love never breaks. It is as strong as the death and resurrection of Jesus.

Study the Good and Evil collage in quiet. 'Father we offer you all the good and evil in the world. Forgive us when we forget ourselves and try to take over from you. Correct us when we try to work without you. Support us when we remember to work with you. Fill us with joy when we get it right.'

Distribute bottles of bubbles. Blow them as high as possible, offering a song or prayers of praise and thanks.

Remembering the Matthew reading, bring people, events and causes before God with the words

Leader   Oh God from you we come,

All   **Let your will be done.**

Stories and other resources

Michael Foreman, *Dinosaurs and All that Rubbish*, Puffin, 1993

Sam McBratney, *Guess How Much I Love You?*, Walker Books, 1994

'Jesus in the Desert', in *Livewires Live* (pp. 40 and 41)

Drama

'Follow the maker's instructions', in *Rap, Rhyme and Reason* (p. 30)

Music

All hail the power of Jesus' name (HAMNS 140, HON 13, HTC 587, SHF 7)

Father hear the prayer we offer (HAMNS 113, HON 120, HTC 360)

Forty days and forty nights (HAMNS 56, HON 145, HTC 103)

God forgave my sin (HON 167, SHF 126)

God made the heavens and earth (BBP 63)

He's got the whole world in his hands (JP 78, JU p. 60)

Jesus is Lord (HON 270, SHF 278)

On the first day of creation (JU p. 68)

Post communion prayer

Lord God,
you have renewed us with the living bread from
    heaven;
by it you nourish our faith,
increase our hope,
and strengthen our love:
teach us always to hunger for him
    who is the true and living bread,
and enable us to live by every word
    that proceeds from out of your mouth;
through Jesus Christ our Lord.

The First Sunday of Lent

The Second Sunday of Lent

 ## Readings

Genesis 12.1-4a

God tells Abram to go to a land promised for him and his descendants. God promises Abram greatness, blessing and protection.

Romans 4.1-5,13-17

The foundation of Abraham's righteousness was primarily in his belief and trust in God. It was not his actions that first brought God's blessing.

John 3.1-17

This is the story of Jesus' conversation with Nicodemus the Pharisee. Nicodemus recognizes truth and integrity in Jesus. Jesus explains to him the importance of being born in the Spirit: a difficult concept for someone brought up in a culture that has come to depend on its religious actions and rituals, rather than to focus on the truths behind them. Faith comes when God is revealed, and God is revealed through Jesus. Salvation comes when the truth of God's love is seen in Jesus.

Collect

Almighty God,
you show to those who are in error the light of
   your truth,
that they may return to the way of righteousness:
grant to all those who are admitted
   into the fellowship of Christ's religion,
that they may reject those things
   that are contrary to their profession,
and follow all such things that are agreeable to
   the same;
through our Lord Jesus Christ,
who is alive and reigns with you,
in the unity of the Holy Spirit,
one God, now and for ever.

 ## Talk/address/ sermon

The Genesis reading is a real challenge. Abram responded to God in faith, taking huge risks. How did he know this really was God's will? What is discernment and from whom can we learn it?

What blessing does God promise Christians today? Freedom from fear, love . . . What does it take for us to accept the gift and get up and go?

Is it easy to differentiate between actions that stem from belief, faith, trust; and those that don't?

Is being born again the same as the penny dropping/everything making sense/things becoming crystal clear? Does it stay like that? What helps to make the penny drop?

 ## Congregational/ group activities

- Demonstrate the difference between a child-like confidence and an adult-like hesitation in trusting God by asking an adult and a child to do something which involves trust, e.g. fall into your arms/go around blindfolded. Point out that Abram trusted God totally, as a child trusts those who love him/her.

- Ask the group to mime the possible responses to a command from God to act in a particular way. This could be fun e.g. the indecisive person; the one who has to prepare 'properly'; the procrastinator; the 'ostrich'; the child who simply gets up and goes.

- Make a 'graffiti wall' with responses to the question, 'So what's so special about Jesus?' Would the penny drop for Nicodemus on hearing these answers?

- Depict a tree 'rooted in trust and faith'. Ask everyone to illustrate fruits that would hang from such a tree.

- Is there a 'land' which God is showing this church? What does God want this church to do? Where is God leading us? What would be 'great' about it?

What blessings would be promised? What protection would we need? Should we just get up and go, like Abram?

- Jesus says that God promises eternal life. What people/places/experiences/relationships would we like to be eternal? This could be a discussion, or people might draw/write silently.

- Ask someone from the congregation who has acted in complete faith to share their experience with everyone through a short interview or personal account.

Prayers/ intercessions

Meditate on the fruits from Activity 4, or the drawings/written materials from Activity 6.

A litany in which world/community/church concerns and delights are brought before God with a versicle and response, e.g.:

Leader Let the whole creation live and love in trust,

All **And may your boundless love become ever clearer.**

Select short phrases from one of the readings to use as prayers or meditation, e.g.

Go from your country to the land that I will show you

I will make you great I will bless you.

Stories and other resources

Arthur Scholey, *Baboushka*, Lion, 1982

J Mortimer, 'Jesus and Nicodemus', in *See What I Mean*, CPAS, 1998

The Children's Illustrated Bible, Dorling Kindersley, 1994

Drama

'Zack rap', in *Rap, Rhyme and Reason* 1996 (p. 9)

Music

Get up out of bed (JU p. 4)

God's love (JU p. 90)

He is Lord, he is Lord (HON 204, HTC 507, JP 75, JU p. 92, SHF 159)

Jubilate, everybody (HON 284, SHF 303)

O praise ye the Lord (HAMNS 203, HON 388, HTC 354, SHF 421)

Spirit of the Living God (HON 454)

Thy hand O God, has guided (HAMNS 171, HON 518, HTC 536)

To God be the glory (HON 522, HTC 584, SHF 559)

Post communion prayer

Almighty God,
you see that we have no power of ourselves to help ourselves:
keep us both outwardly in our bodies,
and inwardly in our souls;
that we may be defended from all adversities which may happen to the body,
and from all evil thoughts which may assault and hurt the soul;
through Jesus Christ our Lord.

The Third Sunday of Lent

 ## Readings

Exodus 17.1-7

As the Israelites journey through the wilderness they become thirsty and anxious, consequently turning against Moses. Moses immediately turns to God for help, angry with the Israelites for testing God in this way. God responds by providing water, but Moses is still troubled by the fact that his people did not trust God.

Romans 5.1-11

Paul believes that faith brings peace and he recognizes a clear link between hope, endurance, character, and yet more hope. The Holy Spirit instils that hope, which is based upon the love of Jesus for everyone, good and bad, shown in his death and resurrection.

John 4.5-42

This is the story of the Samaritan woman at the well, who recognizes Jesus as someone very special, first as a prophet, then as the Messiah. Other Samaritans are brought to faith when they hear and understand Jesus' teaching about spiritual food and drink. These people, normally despised by Jews, recognize God's gift in Jesus. His word speaks to them of truth, and they understand his message. Jesus is driven by his need to finish the task he has been given. He believes that there are many ready to listen, and that his time is limited.

Collect

Almighty God,
whose most dear Son went not up to joy
   but first he suffered pain,
and entered not into glory before he was crucified:
mercifully grant that we, walking in the way of the
   cross,
may find it none other than the way of life and
   peace;
through Jesus Christ your Son our Lord,
who is alive and reigns with you,
in the unity of the Holy Spirit,
one God, now and for ever.

 ## Talk/address/ sermon

Who are those marginalized, even despised by today's society and today's church? What insights have they into the nature of God's love?

John demonstrates how Jesus perceived the urgency of his task. Did Jesus really have a strategy, or was his ministry haphazard and spontaneous?

Losing trust in God and feuding have been continuing characteristics of God's people since Old Testament times. When do we find ourselves testing God? Is it so surprising? What do we need to know to live in peace, trust and harmony?

Reflect on the nature of hope, endurance and character. What is distinctive about Christian hope, endurance and character? Do we have encouraging examples?

John's account shows the universal nature of God's love, and the clarity of his message to those who want to hear it.

 ## Congregational/ group activities

- In groups devise a strategy for proclaiming the Gospel in your parish/workplace/home/school/ etc. How realistic is it?

- Of all the things we quarrel about, which would make God laugh/angry/sad/tearful? When might our quarrels lead to clearer views of God's purpose?

- Share real-life stories of endurance from members of the congregation, the local press, etc.

- Sometimes life's clutter prevents us from seeing God at work in our midst – in everyday, humdrum activities we all pursue. In groups invite each member to identify one aspect of God at work in our midst.

- Prepare one or two volunteers to 'endure' something silly, uncomfortable or tedious, on the understanding that they will get a 'reward'. Can the rest of the congregation identify characteristics of endurance from their observations of this light-hearted exercise?

 ## Prayers/ intercessions

Give thanks for the aspects of God's work identified in Activity 4. Use a versicle and response to link the prayers e.g.

Leader   Oh God help us to see you ever more clearly,

All   **And give thanks for all that you do.**

Bring before God causes for concern in the context of endurance, character and hope.

Give thanks for those who have a clarity of vision – an uncluttered view of God's will in the world, the church and the local community. Pray that we will recognize them and hear them.

Invite children to prepare prayers of their own, to remind the congregation that we don't have to look far for clarity and openness to Jesus' message.

Stories and other resources

Michael Foreman, *The Two Giants*, Hodder and Stoughton, 1967

'Suffering and penitence', in *Children Aloud!*

Lois Rock and Louise Rawlings, *Sad News, Glad News*, Lion, 1997

Drama

Paul McCusker, 'Divisions', in *Fast Food*, Monarch Publications, 1992 (p. 45)

 ## Music

Be still and know (HON 52, SHF 37)

Bind us together, Lord (HON 60, SHF 39)

Come, Lord Jesus, Come (JU p. 88)

Domine Deus (BBP 72)

God's not dead (JU p. 38)

Guide me! O thou great Jehovah (HAMNS 214, HON 188, HTC 528, SHF 144)

How sweet the name of Jesus sounds (HAMNS 122, HON 220, HTC 211, SHF 178)

Let all the world in every corner sing (HAMNS 202, HON 296, HTC 342)

Post communion prayer

Merciful Lord,
grant your people grace to withstand the temptations
   of the world, the flesh and the devil,
and with pure hearts and minds to follow you,
   the only God;
through Jesus Christ our Lord.

Mothering Sunday

The Fourth Sunday of Lent

 ## Readings

Exodus 2.1-10

This is the well-known story of Moses being hidden in the reeds to protect him from Pharaoh's edict to drown all Hebrew boys. Pharaoh's daughter finds the hidden child, employs his mother to nurse the boy and later takes him to be her own son.

or

1 Samuel 1.20-28

This is the story of Hannah who, having prayed for a son, gives birth to Samuel. She then fulfils her own promise to God by placing her newly weaned son into the care of Eli at the Temple.

2 Corinthians 1.3-7

Paul expresses his belief that God consoles those in affliction. The Christians at Corinth must hold on to the idea that any suffering they endure serves to strengthen them as they console others.

or

Colossians 3.12-17

Paul urges the Colossians to be compassionate, kind, humble, meek, forgiving, loving and harmonious. These characteristics are the hallmark of a truly Christian community, where there is also peace, thankfulness, teaching and worship.

Luke 2.33-35

Jesus has just been presented to Simeon at the Temple. His parents are stunned by the old man's reaction to the infant. Simeon recognizes him as one who will bring light to all – and sadness to his parents.

or

John 19.25-27

In this account of Jesus' crucifixion, his mother waits with him until his death. Jesus asks the 'disciple whom he loved' to take his mother into his home.

Collect

God of compassion,
whose Son Jesus Christ, the child of Mary,
shared the life of a home in Nazareth,
and on the cross drew the whole human family to
   himself:
strengthen us in our daily living
that in joy and in sorrow
we may know the power of your presence
   to bind together and to heal;
through Jesus Christ your Son our Lord,
who is alive and reigns with you,
in the unity of the Holy Spirit,
one God, now and for ever.

Talk/address/ sermon

Pharaoh's daughter must have known that the baby was being hidden to escape her father's death warrant, and probably had a good idea that his nurse was his real mother. Sometimes God's purpose is carried out through the most unexpected people! The gift of mothering is not necessarily restricted to those who give birth to children. There are many people who have the gifts of 'mothering'. What are those gifts?

The story of Hannah is a very sharp reminder that no parent owns their child. A parent's only right is to love and care for his/her children in a way that is best for them, and according to God's purpose.

The Corinthians reading raises the huge issue of suffering, and the ways in which suffering serves to strengthen faith, rather than diminish it. Where is the starting point for such a view? What stories do we need to hear/experiences do we need to go through to really understand Paul in this context?

The Colossians reading describes characteristics which together make the hallmark of the obedient Christian community. Families, churches, workplaces and schools might well want to promote those attributes, so often associated with mothers. Why do successive generations think of motherhood in this way? Is this image under threat in our current generation, particularly when men are allowed to have a less macho image and women are sometimes seen as more aggressive?

The two Gospel readings remind us that motherhood was not easy for Mary. Her pregnancy would have been viewed with suspicion. Simeon's response must have been ominous, as well as exciting. In his childhood Jesus probably gave his mother more than her fair share of concern. In his adulthood, she must have known he was heading for trouble. Then at his death she seems to have lost her home as well as her son. The resurrection experience must have been absolutely amazing for her!

Congregational/ group activities

- The story of Moses is one which children might enjoy telling, with previously prepared illustrations.

- Brainstorm characteristics of motherhood as shown by animals towards their young, owners (adults and children) towards their pets, friends towards each other, parents towards their children, and children towards their parents. To what extent do these characteristics correspond with what is described in the Colossians reading?

- Before the service, make a recording of mums of different generations talking about the ups and downs of new/middle/older motherhood. This could take the form of a live interview. Alternatively, ask the friend/relative of a mother who knew her before parenthood, if and how motherhood has changed her.

- Providing as many visual aids as possible, and hastily made labels where necessary, invite everyone to describe the ideal mum by attaching visual aids and labels to a volunteer. Then re-distribute these aids and labels amongst the congregation, reminding everyone that these attributes are ideally those of all people.

- Give groups a large drawing of either the earth or the church. Sometimes people talk of 'Mother Earth' or 'Mother Church'. Why might this be so? Complete the picture in a way that allows other groups  to see what qualities of motherhood your group would associate with the church and our planet.

Prayers/ intercessions

Pile the visual aids and labels from Activity 4 on the altar, maybe re-reading some of the labels. Thank God that all of this, and much more, comes from him.

Use the drawings from Activity 5 to focus upon during a short time of meditation.

Thank God for the rescue of Moses and what it teaches us about God's unexpected ways of working.

Thank God for all the mothering that is given by those who have not given birth to children and for all those men, women and children who have shown motherly love to us.

 ## Stories and other resources

Donald Dowling, 'Ta Ma or soft soap – a myth retold', in *Together for Festivals*

Kahlil Gibran, 'Speak to us of children . . .', in *The Prophet,* Paperback Pan Books, 1991 (p. 22)

'God, man and woman', in *Wild Goose Prints No. 2,* Wild Goose Publications 1986 (p. 34)

Robert Munsch, *Love You Forever,* Firefly, 1988

Jean Thomson, 'Activities for Mothering Sunday', in *Together for Festivals*

'My little brother', in *Best Friends*

 ## Drama

Paul McCusker, 'Dad's hotline', in *Fast Food,* Monarch, 1992

'As a mother . . . ', in *Plays for all Seasons*

 ## Music

All over the world (HON 16)

A new commandment (HON 4, SHF 14)

For the beauty of the earth (HAMNS 104, HON 137, HTC 298)

I am a new creation (HON 221)

Jesus, good above all other (HAMNS 378, HON 269, HTC 96)

Living under the shadow of his wing (SHF 331)

Make me a channel of your peace (HON 328)

Now thank we all our God (HAMNS 205, HON 354, HTC 33)

Post communion prayer

Loving God,
as a mother feeds her children at the breast
you feed us in this sacrament
    with the food and drink of eternal life:
help us who have tasted your goodness
to grow in grace within the household of faith;
through Jesus Christ our Lord.

Mothering Sunday

The Fifth Sunday of Lent

 ## Readings

Ezekiel 37.1-14

This is the story of Ezekiel's vision of the valley of dry bones. Before his own eyes, and through words put into his mouth by the Lord, the bones of a multitude of slain Israelites are brought back to life. This vision is to encourage the exiled people of Israel, cut off from their homeland, dispersed and without hope. God uses Ezekiel to promise them that they will return home and live as his chosen people.

Romans 8.6-11

If we cannot see beyond the physical reality of life, we are not living fully. Indeed, by not recognizing the significance of the spiritual dimension, we are working against it. Those for whom Christ's love is real are those who are fully alive in the Spirit.

John 11.1-45

Lazarus, a friend of Jesus, is very ill in Judaea. His sisters send for Jesus, who does not set out immediately to visit his friend. When, after two days, he finally announces his intention to go, his disciples are anxious: Jesus is not popular with the authorities in Judaea and his life is already in danger. However Jesus believes that his return will signal an event which will bring more people to belief in him. When he reaches the house Lazarus has died and Mary and Martha are very upset at the delay in his coming, believing that his presence would have saved their brother. Jesus is moved to tears by their grief, but still sees this event as an opportunity for God to reveal himself to more people. He prays that God will raise Lazarus and when it happens, many are brought to faith.

Collect

Most merciful God,
who by the death and resurrection of your Son
    Jesus Christ
delivered and saved the world:
grant that by faith in him who suffered on the
    cross
we may triumph in the power of his victory;
through Jesus Christ your Son our Lord,
who is alive and reigns with you,
in the unity of the Holy Spirit,
one God, now and for ever.

 ## Talk/address/ sermon

We are much more than flesh and bone. We are creatures of the eternal God: when we really see that, then we live fully. It is as though we see the 'bigger picture'.

Surrounding ourselves with things of the world: money, possessions, activities, friendships, etc. does not in itself bring life in abundance, because we know that all these things can be lost. These same things are good and precious, yet their value is so much greater when we realize that they are within the context of the love of God which we can never lose.

In the Gospel reading Jesus is disturbed by the death of his friend, and yet regards the whole incident as significant in God's purpose. Perhaps he recognizes his own frightening fate and, through the raising of Lazarus, is reassured of God's will for him.

The sense of Jesus having a very specific task to fulfil within a particular time-scale is evident again in the Gospel reading, which touches many issues. Is Jesus frightened about his future? He has the faith to know God will act, but does he really know that Lazarus will rise again? Mary and Martha are convinced that his presence alone is guarantee enough! Whilst Jesus longs for his friend's life, he sees Lazarus' resurrection primarily as a means of God teaching people about his loving purpose.

Congregational/ group activities

- With Ezekiel in mind prepare a mime: stiff, lifeless puppets with fixed smiles and stares are transformed into warm, laughing, living beings as they are 'inspired' by God to remember that they are his creatures.

- Act out an advert with Miss 'Got it all', acquiring things, people and wild experiences. In the background is the silent figure on the cross. Everything belonging to Miss 'Got it all' begins to wear out/disappear, upsetting her, but clearing her vision of the cross. In her distress she suddenly 'sees' the figure and the cross more clearly; realizing the truth, she sweeps the remaining things to one side, as the figure from the cross comes out to embrace her. Then, together and carefully, they retrieve what she has discarded and put all the things, experiences and people in their 'proper' places i.e. in the context of God's love.

- Ask people of all ages to describe one aspect of the truth of God's love that they know for themselves. What difference does it make to them? Do they ever need reminding that they are God's son/ daughter?

 ## Prayers/ intercessions

Use Psalm 139.1-4 and 13-14 (and perhaps present appropriate slides too) as a basis for prayers which remind us that we belong in God's love.

Versicle and response for prayers of thanksgiving

Leader In your generosity,

All **Help us to see you, O Lord.**

Versicle and response for prayers of intercession

Leader In your generosity,

All **Help us to trust you, O Lord.**

Versicle and response for prayers of confession

Leader In your generosity,

All **Help us to thank you, O Lord.**

Versicle and response for prayers of praise

Leader In your generosity,

All **Help us to praise you, O Lord.**

 ## Stories and other resources

John L. Bell, 'Lazarus', in *He was in the World*, Wild Goose Publications, 1995 (p. 77)

'Lazarus', in *Building New Bridges* (p. 100)

 ## Drama

Derek Haylock, 'A grave business', in *Sketches from Scripture*, NS/CHP, 1992

♪ ♫ ♪ ♪ ♩ ♪♫ Music

It is a thing most wonderful (HAMNS 70, HON 255, HTC 131)

Jesus is my friend (BBP 78)

Lead us, heavenly Father, lead us (HAMNS 224, HON 293, HTC 525, SHF 306)

O for a thousand tongues to sing (HAMNS 125, HON 362, HTC 219, SHF 394)

Rejoice in the Lord always (HON 430, SHF 462)

Rejoice! Rejoice! (SHF 461)

Post communion prayer

Lord Jesus Christ,
you have taught us
that what we do for the least of our brothers and sisters
we do also for you:
give us the will to be the servant of others
as you were the servant of all,
and gave up your life and died for us,
but are alive and reign, now and for ever.

Palm Sunday

 ## Readings

Liturgy of the Palms

Matthew 21.1-11

Jesus sends two disciples into Jerusalem with clear and simple instructions. As if he knows exactly what is expected of him, the owner of the donkey hands both the donkey and the colt over without hesitation. Jesus has made a huge impression upon the crowds that have gathered, and accepts their adulation as though it were inevitable. The impact of his arrival and the crowd's response cause turmoil in the city.

Liturgy of the Passion

Isaiah 50.4-9a

The book of Isaiah tells of a teacher (the Suffering Servant) whom God inspires to uplift the weary, even though he brings suffering upon himself as a consequence. God helps him in his task and this gives him strength to carry on, for he is convinced that in the end no one can defeat God.

Philippians 2.5-11

Paul summarizes the amazing truth of the Incarnation. God becomes fully human in Jesus so that his love will be known by all people. This leads to his death, but God's realm is bigger than mortal life, so Jesus' death is overcome and his deity is recognized.

Matthew 26.14 – 27.66

Judas agrees with the chief priests that he will betray Jesus in exchange for money. Jesus and the disciples then share in the Passover meal where Jesus makes it clear to Judas that he knows he is to be betrayed by him. He goes on to share bread and wine, speaking as though the disciples share in his life and death, and as though they will not share another meal together until after his death. We are then taken to the trial before the high priests who accuse Jesus of blasphemy and demand his death.

or

Matthew 27.11-54

This is a very detailed account of the trial before Pilate, the uncertainty of Pilate, the freeing of Barabbas and the horrible proceedings that lead to Jesus' crucifixion.

There is darkness and earthquake at the time of his death and, in their terror, those Roman soldiers who carry out the orders of their leaders in executing Jesus are sure that he is of celestial significance.

Collect

> Almighty and everlasting God,
> who in your tender love towards the human race
>   sent your Son our Saviour Jesus Christ
> to take upon him our flesh
> and to suffer death upon the cross:
> grant that we may follow the example
> of his patience and humility,
> and also be made partakers of his resurrection;
> through Jesus Christ your Son our Lord,
> who is alive and reigns with you,
> in the unity of the Holy Spirit,
> one God, now and for ever.

 ## Talk/address/ sermon

The Isaiah reading shows the strength of real conviction and how a total confidence in God sustains the believer, no matter what. What is the conviction that sustains Jesus during the terrible time of his death?

Why does Jesus cause so much turmoil? The impact of his teaching brings ultimate joy to some and fear to others. He is loved and he is hated. To whom is he a joy and to whom a threat?

Jesus' solemn awareness of his fate, which has been a feature of the Gospel readings during these last few weeks, continues through to his death. He seems to realize that the authorities will never understand his Messiahship and to argue for God will be pointless. It is almost as though he sorrows for them in their futile fear. He does not seem at all surprised that the crowds who cheered him into the city are as united in their cry to have him killed.

There is an 'otherness' about Jesus that un-nerves Pilate and an atmosphere at the time of his death that affects the Roman soldiers. The people on the edge of Jewish life have more than a hint of his real identity, whilst those who should have been the first to recognize him fail to do so.

Congregational/ group activities

- Show an extract of a film depicting any of the Gospel readings. Stop it at an appropriate point and ask what happens next. Alternatively, ask people to get into groups and remember together the Gospel accounts without referring to the Bible. Then have the Gospel read aloud and see how well the groups have remembered this very important story.

- Tell the Gospel story through the eyes of Simon of Cyrene, a Roman soldier, Barabbas (or his wife/son/daughter) or any of the many onlookers of this final week of Jesus' life.

- Decorate home-made cloaks, pieces of cloth and palm leaves with words of praise, and make a trail with them to the cross.

- What is a goody-goody/do-gooder? Is there a difference between such a person and a person of truth and integrity? Why do we sometimes resent people of truth and integrity, and what can we learn about ourselves from the behaviour of the Jews towards Jesus?

 ## Prayers/ intercessions

Use phrases or words from the readings to link prayers for the day e.g.

'Truly this man was God's Son'

'Hosanna to the Son of David'

'Morning by morning he wakens my ear . . .'

Give thanks for those who regard Christianity as a joy; pray for those for whom it is a threat. Contact Release International, Amnesty International, etc. for information about those who suffer for their faith.

On the reverse side of the home-made palms and cloaks add names, causes, newspaper cuttings etc., which people want to pray for and replace them on a path to the cross.

 ## Stories and other resources

Building New Bridges (pp. 74–77)

'Holy week and Easter', in *Children Celebrate!* (p. 71, 77–86)

'Making an entry', in *Livewires Live*

Ian Macleod (ed.), *Even More Talks for Children*, St Andrews Press, 1997

 ## Drama

'Betrayal – Judas', in *Rap, Rhyme and Reason* (p. 93)

'Kisses', in *Rap, Rhyme and Reason* (p. 49)

'On trial', in *Plays for all Seasons* (p. 49)

 ## Music

All glory laud and honour (HAMNS 60, HON 11, HTC 120)

From heaven you came (HON 148, SHF 120)

God's not dead (JU p. 38)

Hail to the Lord's anointed (HAMNS 142, HON 193, HTC 190, SHF 146)

Hosanna, hosanna (BBP 38)

Make way, make way (HON 329)

Ride on, ride on in majesty (HAMNS 61, HON 435, HTC 119)

We are marching in the light of God (JU p. 34)

When I'm feeling down and sad (BBP 74)

Post communion prayer

Lord Jesus Christ,
you humbled yourself in taking the form of a
    servant,
and in obedience died on the cross for our
    salvation:
give us the mind to follow you
and to proclaim you as Lord and King,
to the glory of God the Father

Easter Day

 ## Readings

Acts 10.34-43

Peter, speaking in house of Cornelius, a Roman centurion, tells how he witnessed the life, crucifixion and resurrection of Jesus. Indeed, he is a chosen witness, charged to preach God's forgiveness to all people through Jesus. This forgiveness is for all: God accepts all people who fear him.

or

Jeremiah 31.1-6

The Lord has an everlasting love for his people. His people will be rebuilt and the day will come when they shall say, 'Come, let us go up to Zion, to the Lord our God'.

Colossians 3.1-4

In writing of 'things above' Paul refers to the ancient concept of the higher and lower worlds between which humanity must choose. However, by the time Paul was writing, Jewish thought had interpreted this idea as 'the present age', and 'the age to come' and this understanding passed into Christian understanding also. Paul assures his readers that for those who set their hearts on the age to come, the resurrection makes all the difference.

John 20.1-18

Mary Magdalene discovers the empty tomb and returns to share the news with Simon Peter and the other disciple who go to the tomb and discover the burial cloths, confirming what Mary has said. They leave again but Mary remains at the tomb weeping and it is to her that Jesus appears, commanding her to go and tell the others.

or

Matthew 28.1-10

When the two Marys visit the tomb of Jesus, they are told by an angel to 'Come, see the place where he lay'. They are told to return to the disciples and to tell them that Jesus has risen from the dead. Suddenly, Jesus appears and greets them and they worship him.

Collect

Lord of all life and power,
who through the mighty resurrection of your Son
overcame the old order of sin and death
to make all things new in him:
grant that we, being dead to sin
and alive to you in Jesus Christ,
may reign with him in glory;
to whom with you and the Holy Spirit
be praise and honour, glory and might,
now and in all eternity.

 ## Talk/address/ sermon

The resurrection is about faith – but it is also about action. It is to Mary, the one who faithfully waits at the tomb, that Jesus appears. Her action, of faithfulness even to the grave, is one on which we have reflected in the events of Holy Week, for as the Church we keep faith, even when it means confronting sadness and pain. But our reward reflects that of Mary – we experience the joy of the resurrection, not as something we can explain, but as something we know. And because we know it, we must act upon it. Jesus charges Mary to go and tell the disciples. Her fear is transformed into joy, but with it comes the responsibility of action. We too, in the joy which we experience on Easter day, are witnesses of the resurrection, and with our joy comes the responsibility of action. Peter, speaking in the house of Cornelius, the Roman centurion, tells of his new understanding that through Jesus, acceptance by God is for all people. As witnesses of the resurrection, the disciples are entrusted with the task of sharing that good news of forgiveness with all. We too are witnesses of the resurrection today and as witnesses, we share that task.

 ## Congregational/ group activities

- Make resurrection eggs to take home and keep throughout Eastertide as a celebration of Easter joy. Use whole egg shells from which the contents have been emptied through a small window in the front. Dye them or spray them gold. Glue round the front

'window' and edge it with a piece of gold cord or with glitter. Fill the bottom of the shell with damp sand or cotton wool. Make a tiny empty cross out of pieces of cocktail stick sprayed gold, bind it with coloured thread or a piece of fine fuse wire and stand it in the damp material in the egg. Finally add two or three tiny flowers, for example violets or primula heads. These can be replaced as required as the Easter season progresses. Celandines, buttercups and daisies and pieces of aubretia will all be suitable and are readily available. If you can't get real flowers you could use fabric ones (you may need to take bought sprays apart) or use sugar flowers bought in cake icing sets).

- Make up a simple Easter dance. Carols were originally dance tunes and used to be associated with Easter as well as Christmas. There are several Easter carols in the Oxford Book of Carols, which provide good dance tunes. From the hymn books you could use 'Now the green blade riseth'. Use yellow and green ribbons and perhaps some simple percussion instruments to enhance the rhythm of the tune you select. Create a simple circle dance to illustrate the carol's words.

- Begin to create a series showing *Experiences of the Resurrection*. You could either make a six page book or six 'stations' somewhere in the church, perhaps on the window sills. This week's witness is Mary Magdalene. Put her words onto a scroll or book page for everyone to see 'Mary Magdalene went to the disciples with the news: "I have seen the Lord!"' Then add visuals in whatever way is appropriate. You could include a folded white cloth, jars of spices, a pathway and plants in a church-based station. In a book people may like to draw these, or draw Mary encountering Jesus in the garden.

Prayers/ intercessions

Use the Eastertide intercession on page 278 of *Lent, Holy Week and Easter.* If it is possible stand around the church's Easter garden for these prayers. The following symbols may be presented to the leader of the intercessions before each petition and then placed at the entrance to the empty tomb as the congregational response is made:

We praise you for the resurrection: *a lighted candle*

We pray for those who at this season are receiving baptism: *a small flask of water*

We pray for all whom we know and love: *a jar of spices or ointment*

We pray for those who suffer pain and anguish: *a piece of white fabric tied up with a red ribbon*

We remember before you those who have died in the hope of the resurrection: *a crown of thorns bound together with a piece of gold ribbon or tinsel.*

Stories and other resources

Caryll Houselander, *Petook, An Easter Story*, Burns and Oates/Collins Dove, 1990

Brian Wildsmith, *The Easter Story*, Oxford University Press, 1993

Frances Hodgson Burnett, *The Secret Garden* (Chapter 9), Penguin, 1995

Leslie Francis and Nicola Slee, *The Sunny Morning: Teddy Horsley Celebrates the New Life of Easter*, NCEC, 1984

Margaret Cooling and Jane Taylor, *Ten Minute Miracle Plays for Easter*, Bible Society, 1995

'The light that would not blow out' in *Celebration!*

Bob Hartman, 'The angel of death and life', in *Angels Angels All Around*, Lion, 1993

The Complete Children's Liturgy Book (p.48)

'Resurrection', in *Pick and Mix* (p.148)

Drama

Ruth Tiller, *Keeping the Feast*, Kevin Mayhew (Easter Sunday: 'We are an Easter people' p. 24, 'Knowing what to think' p. 27)

Music

Alleluia, alleluia give thanks to the risen Lord (HON 24, SHF 5)

All in an Easter garden (CP 130)

Christ the Lord is risen again (HAMNS 79, HON 80, HTC 153)

Easter tells us (BBP 41)

'Happy Easter' we will say (BBP 44)

Jesus Christ is risen today (HAMNS 77, HON 267, HTC 155, SHF 269)

Lord of the morning (WGS 2, p. 62)

The day of resurrection (HAMNS 75, HON 474, HTC 161)

Post communion prayer

God of Life,
who for our redemption gave your only-begotten Son
    to the death of the cross,
and by his glorious resurrection
have delivered us from the power of our enemy:
grant us so to die daily to sin,
that we may evermore live with him
    in the joy of his risen life;
through Jesus Christ our Lord.

The Second Sunday of Easter

 ## Readings

Exodus 14.10-31; 15.20-21*

The Lord provides an escape route for Moses and the Israelites across the Red Sea and destroys Pharaoh's pursuing army.

* If the Old Testament reading is used on Sundays in Eastertide, the reading from Acts must be used as the second reading.

Acts 2.14a,22-32

Peter, speaking to the crowd on the day of Pentecost, assures them that Jesus, whose life was marked by signs of God's work, was crucified and rose again, reflecting the words of David in Psalm 16.

1 Peter 1.3-9

The writer assures his readers that the great faith which they hold, and which has resulted in their persecution, will nevertheless lead them into a wonderful inheritance, which they cannot ultimately be denied.

John 20.19-31

There has been no doubt, from the earliest days of the Church, that it is the power of the Spirit that enables people to do the work of God. Here Jesus, appearing to his fearful disciples who had locked themselves away, sends them out with the power of the Spirit. Thomas, not present with the others, finds it hard to believe their story and Jesus appears to him on another occasion, prompting a significant confession of faith, that Jesus is 'My Lord and my God!'. But Jesus reassures those who, like us, have not been visual witnesses, that they are blessed through their faith.

Collect

Almighty Father,
you have given your only Son to die for our sins
and to rise again for our justification:
grant us so to put away the leaven of malice and
  wickedness
that we may always serve you
in pureness of living and truth;
through the merits of your Son Jesus Christ our Lord,
who is alive and reigns with you
in the unity of the Holy Spirit,
one God, now and for ever.

 ## Talk/address/ sermon

Blindfold a volunteer from the congregation and give them a number of objects in turn to feel (such as an orange, a book, a teddy bear, or some unusual household items such as a garlic press or a potato peeler). Can they guess what the object is without seeing it? Discuss the difficulty of not being able to know for sure what was there without seeing it, but how they could be fairly certain by using a number of clues – such as feeling or smelling the object.

In the gospel reading Thomas will not believe in Jesus unless he has seen and touched him for himself. Yet many people throughout the centuries have believed in the risen Christ for themselves, without having the evidence that was given to Thomas. What 'clues' are we given to the resurrection of Christ? What does Jesus say about those who believe and know the reality of Jesus' spiritual presence, but have never seen him physically?

 ## Congregational/ group activities

- The gospel writer states his purpose in recording the signs of Jesus in the presence of his disciples: 'these are written that you may believe that Jesus is the Christ, the Son of God, and that by believing you may have life in his name'. In groups, discuss events that have made a momentous difference in your lives; and tell each other of things that have 'helped you to believe'.

- Make resurrection cards. Fold a piece of A4 card in half and on the front section draw three doors. Cut these on three sides so that they will open. On the front write the words 'We believe'. Inside the doors write 'Receive the Holy Spirit', 'Peace be with you' and 'My Lord and my God!'. Decorate the doors and the area around them on the front of the card and inside illustrate the story of the disciples and Thomas meeting with the risen Christ. Older

children will be able to make the whole card themselves, younger children will need parts of it to be started for them.

- Make the second station or page of *Experiences of the Resurrection*. This week's witness is Thomas. Put these words onto a scroll or book page: 'Thomas said to him, "My Lord and my God!" Then Jesus told him, "Have you believed because you have seen me? Blessed are those who have not seen and yet have come to believe."' The visual symbols could be a door with a key in it (even the locked door could not prevent Jesus from reaching his fearful disciples and doubting Thomas) and some large nails, reminding us of the marks in Jesus' hands. You could put the words 'Peace be with you' on the door. In a book people may like to draw Thomas greeting Jesus and Jesus greeting the disciples. Under the pictures you may like to add the words from the Gospel: 'these are written that you may believe that Jesus is the Christ, the Son of God, and that by believing you may have life in his name.'

Prayers/intercessions

Christ, who stood among the disciples,
showing them your hands and feet
to take away their doubts,
We welcome you.

Christ, who met with the disciples,
eating in their presence
to make them see,
We welcome you.

Christ who spoke to the disciples,
opening their minds
to reveal God's promise
We welcome you.

You,
who stand among us,
meet with us,
speak to us,
Have mercy on us.

If we are ruled by doubt, have mercy on us,
Have mercy on us.
If we live in fear, as if you are still dead,
Have mercy on us.
If we fail to be your hands and feet,
Have mercy on us.
If we read Scripture but do not grasp the Gospel,
Have mercy on us.
If we do not forgive as we are forgiven,
Have mercy on us.

Silence

We receive the gift of grace, from him who promised grace,
We receive the gift of peace, from him who promised peace
We receive the gift of life, from him who died and lives again.
Thanks be to God.

> Francis Brienen, from Maureen Edwards (comp.), *More Living Prayers for Today*, IBRA, 1997

Stories and other resources

The Complete Children's Liturgy Book (p. 50)

Margaret Dean, 'Resurrection', in *Pick and Mix* (p. 148)

50 Five Minute Stories

Sue Relf, *100 Instant Ideas for All-Age Worship*, Kingsway, 1998

Drama

'Easter drama', in *Children Aloud!* (p. 58)

Music

Among us and before us (HON 28)

He is Lord (HON 204, SHF 159)

I give you all the honour (HON 230)

Jesus in the garden (CP 129)

Love's redeeming work is done (HAMNS 83, HON 324)

My daughters and my sons (SS 48)

These things did Thomas (SS 49)

Post communion prayer

Lord God our Father,
through our Saviour Jesus Christ
you have assured your children of eternal life
and in baptism have made us one with him:
deliver us from the death of sin
and raise us to new life in your love,
in the fellowship of the Holy Spirit,
by the grace of our Lord Jesus Christ.

The Third Sunday of Easter

 ## Readings

Zephaniah 3.14-20

Zion is told to rejoice, for the Lord has overcome their enemies. He will gather together his scattered people and will restore their esteem and prosperity.

Acts 2.14a,36-41

This is an account of how the rapid growth of the Church followed the testimony of the witnesses of the resurrection. Peter continues to address the crowd on the day of Pentecost and to witness to the fact that the forgiveness of sins and the promise of the Holy Spirit is for them and for all who are far away. Through repentance and baptism in the name of Jesus, they will receive forgiveness. Three thousand people are baptized and the rapid growth of the Church has begun.

1 Peter 1.17-23

The writer describes the consequences of belief in the resurrection. Those who are able to call God 'Father' must remember that their redemption has been costly, through the death of Christ.

Luke 24.13-35

The story of Jesus joining the two disciples on the road to Emmaus appears only in Luke's gospel. Two disciples are travelling from Jerusalem to Emmaus talking about all that has happened, when they are joined by a stranger who explains the significance of events to them. It is only when, on arriving at their destination, they press their hospitality on the stranger, that he reveals himself to them as Jesus, when he breaks the bread.

Collect

Almighty Father,
who in your great mercy gladdened the disciples
   with the sight of the risen Lord:
give us such knowledge of his presence with us,
that we may be strengthened and sustained
   by his risen life
and serve you continually in righteousness and
   truth;
through Jesus Christ your Son our Lord,
who is alive and reigns with you,
in the unity of the Holy Spirit,
one God, now and for ever.

 ## Talk/address/sermon

The records of the resurrection in the Gospels are particularly diverse, reflecting the diversity of the experiences of those who encountered the risen Christ. The moving story of the disciples on the road to Emmaus may echo our own experience: so often we are unaware of God's presence. We go about what we have to do, we concern ourselves with our own worries and problems. It is only when we stop and reflect, or maybe when we notice the needs of another, that we are aware of God's presence. We all have different experiences, we need to reflect on them and share them. For it is often in sharing with one another that we are enabled to understand what has happened.

 ## Congregational/group activities

- Send people out in pairs for a walk for about five minutes. Ask them to talk together of thoughts, sentiments and feelings about the resurrection or of a sad or empty time in their life and someone who cared for them then or who brought hope in their sadness. When they come back into the church, they might join up with another pair and share the discussions they had. Those who are not able to go out could stay in pairs inside. This activity would be best undertaken **before** the Gospel is read.

- Display on a table the following things: a model or picture of a crown, a wedding ring, a dove, a cross, the word 'alleluia', a spring flower and an egg. Ask people to talk about what each item makes them think of. With a group of children, they might each be invited to select an item in turn. When this is completed, put bread and wine on the table and ask people to talk again of what they think of when they see it and why. Then read or tell the Gospel story.

- Make the third station or page of *Experiences of the Resurrection*. Use the words 'Stay with us, for it is nearly evening; the day is almost over' and 'Were not our hearts burning within us while he talked with us on the road and opened the Scriptures to us?' Add bread and wine as the main visual items. A path leading away from a city, perhaps with three people walking along it, may also be added.

Prayers/ intercessions

O unfamiliar God,
we seek you in the places
you have already left,
and fail to see you
even when you stand before us.
Grant us so to recognise your strangeness
that we need not cling to our familiar grief,
but may be freed to proclaim your resurrection
in the name of Christ, Amen

Janet Morley, from Maureen Edwards (comp.),
More Living Prayers for Today, IBRA, 1997 (p. 83)

A response for intercessions may reflect this prayer:

Leader   O God, stand before us;

All   **Free us to proclaim your resurrection.**

Stories and other resources

Stefan's prisoner by Jenny Robertson and *The Sharing bread* by Arthur Scholey, in Pat Alexander, *Song of the Morning, Easter Stories and Poems for Children*, Lion, 1997

The Complete Children's Liturgy Book (p. 52)

Lois Rock and Louise Rawlings, *Sad News, Glad News*, Lion, 1997

Drama

Sheila Ward Ling 'The resurrection', in *Together for Festivals*

'Easter tableaux', in *Children Aloud!*

Music

'A butterfly, an Easter egg' in *The Children's Hymn Book*, Kevin Mayhew, 1997 (p. 1)

Easter Evening (WGS 2, p. 76)

From hand to hand (BBP 55)

I am the bread of life (HON 222, HTC 5.10, SHF 182)

Jesus stand among us in thy risen power (HON 280, HTC 364, SHF 291)

Now the green blade riseth (HAMNS 501, HON 355)

Stay with us (MT2 p. 69)

The sharing bread (CP 139) This song goes with the story of *The Sharing Bread* by Arthur Scholey suggested above.

The strife is past (HAMNS 78, HON 495, HTC 163)

The time was early evening (SS 33)

Post communion prayer

Living God,
your Son made himself known to his disciples
in the breaking of bread:
open the eyes of our faith,
that we may see him in all his redeeming work;
who is alive and reigns, now and for ever.

The Fourth Sunday of Easter

 ## Readings

Genesis 7

This extended reading gives the full account of the story of Noah: from the command to build the ark, to the forty-day flood and the destruction of all living things outside the boat.

Acts 2.42-47

Luke gives a description of the lifestyle of the first believers. Breaking bread together was clearly significant for it is mentioned twice. They worshipped daily, their communal life was important and their numbers grew.

1 Peter 2.19-25

The writer assures his readers that when they suffer pain and injustice, they follow in the steps of Christ, who suffered for us. He is like the shepherd to sheep who are going astray.

John 10.1-10

Jesus is talking to his disciples before the crucifixion and uses an image which recurs in ancient literature, that of a shepherd caring for his sheep. Shepherds were familiar figures in first century Palestine and walked ahead of their flocks, knowing each individual animal and using a special call with which the sheep would be familiar. When they needed protection, the flock would be taken into a walled courtyard and a door keeper would keep them fastened in until the shepherd returned. If a thief broke in, he would not be able to take out the flock and keep it together, for the sheep would not know his voice and as soon as they were free would scatter and wander away.

Collect

Almighty God,
whose Son Jesus Christ is the resurrection and
   the life:
raise us, who trust in him,
from the death of sin to the life of righteousness,
that we may seek those things which are above,
where he reigns with you
in the unity of the Holy Spirit,
one God, now and for ever.

 ## Talk/address/ sermon

Stories about shepherds and sheep pervade the Bible. Jacob looked after Laban's sheep, Moses looked after Jethro's. Psalm 23 likens God to a shepherd. The shepherds are the witnesses to the birth of Jesus. Shepherds were a vital part of the economy in the community in which Jesus lived and in the community where John wrote his Gospel. Yet their work was hard and required enormous care and commitment. Day and night, whatever the circumstances, the sheep required their care. It was individual care: the sheep knew the shepherd's voice, and his touch, and he knew them. He could identify even one missing animal. If he left them, it was locked up safely somewhere. Yet when he roamed the hills and valleys searching for pasture, the sheep remained close to the shepherd and followed him. He was the key to their safety and well-being. There was no substitute. In the passage from St John's Gospel, Jesus tells his disciples that his care for humanity is like that of a shepherd for his sheep. It is individual, constant and unique. As the shepherd is the key to the well-being and safety of his sheep, so Jesus is the key to fullness of life.

Congregational/ group activities

- Hide some little toy sheep (they could be plastic farm animals or knitted toys or simply paper cutouts) around the church and invite children to hunt and find them all. Make sure they are all found: you will need to know how many were put out! If the last few prove hard to find, provide sufficient clues but work hard at the search. Gather all the sheep into a sheepfold and supply a shepherd for them. Talk about what the shepherd will be like. Give one person a shepherd's crook (make it out of a cane and bent wire if you can't get a real one) and let him or her lead a group of children on a walk around the church or, better still, outside. Talk about the experiences of leading and of being led.

- Have copies of the Gospel text for people to look at. Discuss the image of the shepherd used by Jesus in John 10. What is good about it? Can people think of times when the image has been particularly meaningful or relevant to them? And what about the statement 'I have come that they may

have life, and have it to the full'. What does each person think 'fullness of life' is?

- Make the fourth station or page of *Experiences of the Resurrection*. Use the words 'I am the gate; whoever enters through me will be saved. I have come that they may have life, and have it to the full.' Visual material can include a flock of sheep following a shepherd, created in whatever way is available to you; a gate standing open, perhaps to a sheep pen and Jesus standing beside it or a picture of Jesus welcoming people. You may also like to include a shepherd's crook as a symbol of the shepherd's care for his flock.

Prayers/ intercessions

Use the Resurrection intercession on page 72 of *Patterns for Worship*. Those who would like to contribute could be given a sheep shape cut out of paper on which they may write particular concerns for which they would like to offer prayers. At the appropriate petition, the sheep may be placed in a basket representing a sheepfold, so symbolically gathering all the concerns to the care of the Good Shepherd.

Lord Jesus, the Good Shepherd,
you look for those who have strayed and are lost;
look after our lives so that we become your friends
and stay close to you today and for ever.
Amen.

Prayers for Children (p. 200)

Stories and other resources

'The good shepherd', in *Celebration!*

The Complete Children's Liturgy Book (p. 54)

Lesley and Neil Pinchbeck, *Theme Fun*, Scripture Union, 1995 (pp. 27–28)

Prayers for Children (p. 200)

 ## Drama

'Follow the leader', in *Plays on the Word*

 ## Music

Loving shepherd of thy sheep ((HAMNS 134, HON 325, HTC 305)

One more step along the world I go (HON 405, CP 47)

The King of love (HAMNS 126, HON 484, HTC 44, SHF 513)

The Lord's my shepherd (HAMNS 426, HON 490, HTC 591, SHF 526)

The Lord, the Lord, the Lord is my shepherd (BBP 19, CP 108)

This little light of mine (HON 510)

Were you there when they crucified my Lord? (HON 540)

Wherever you go I will follow (BBP 16)

Post communion prayer

Merciful Father,
you gave your Son Jesus Christ to be the good shepherd,
and in his love for us to lay down his life and rise again:
keep us always under his protection,
and give us grace to follow in his steps;
through Jesus Christ our Lord.

The Fifth Sunday of Easter

 ## Readings

Genesis 8.1-19

The story of Noah continues. The forty-day flood comes to an end and the ark comes to rest on the mountains of Ararat.

Acts 7.55-60

This is an account of the first Christian martyrdom. In Acts chapter 6 we read that Stephen, a man full of faith and the Holy Spirit, is chosen with six others to care for the needy among the Christian community. He soon attracts attention for his goodness and wisdom and is brought before the Jewish Council where he defends his faith. As a result he is taken out of the city and stoned. The young man named Saul, who held the clothes, became Paul, the apostle, whose preaching of the Gospel we shall encounter next week.

1 Peter 2.2-10

This passage includes two powerful images. Milk is pure food, provided for the most vulnerable young creatures. And then we meet the image of the stone. Jesus himself, quoting Psalm 118, had suggested he was the 'stone which the builders rejected' which became 'the main corner-stone'. Members of the Church are to be 'living stones', building a living community, held together by Christ, the most important stone of all.

John 14.1-14

This forms part of John's account of Jesus' teaching at the Last Supper. The passage begins by echoing the spirituality of the Psalms: Jesus' teaching is influenced at its heart by the Jewish tradition in which he grew up. The questions of the two disciples reflect this also and their questions reveal their perplexity about who Jesus is. Jesus uses their questions to provide one of his powerful teachings, 'I am the way, the truth and the life'.

Collect

Almighty God,
who through your only-begotten Son Jesus Christ
have overcome death and opened to us
   the gate of everlasting life:
grant that, as by your grace going before us
   you put into our minds good desires,
so by your continual help
we may bring them to good effect;
through Jesus Christ our risen Lord,
who is alive and reigns with you,
in the unity of the Holy Spirit,
one God, now and for ever.

 ## Talk/address/ sermon

Use a glass of milk (or even a baby's bottle) and a large, solid stone (preferably a piece of building stone – if this is not available, you could use a brick instead) to help people to think about the passage from 1 Peter. Milk is the first food we have. It is a basic building block of life in the first few months of our independent existence. It is pure and should be completely safe. A stone is very different. It is solid, and if a part of a building, can contribute to our protection against the cold, the wet, the heat and even, sometimes, more sinister dangers. But wrongly used it can be dangerous. A carelessly built wall may fall, exposing us to injury. The juxtaposition of the images is peculiar and therefore striking. Being concerned for our inward and spiritual nurture enables us to be active, living and supportive members of God's living community which is held together by Christ, the most important stone of all.

 ## Congregational/ group activities

- Try building adjacent walls with Lego or Duplo bricks. Work out how to hold a corner together really well. If you have several groups you may like to compare efforts and test them to find which are the most effective structures. Then look at the reading from 1 Peter 2. Why do people think that the writer chose these particular words from Isaiah to describe Jesus? How are they helpful to us?

- Think about and celebrate difference: identify ways in which people are different and record these. If there is sufficient time, you might write qualities on simple pin or stick figure shapes of different sizes and colours. Here are a few to start you off: small, tall, old, young, musical, artistic, sporty, thoughtful, kind, African, Italian, British, American, dark, fair, quiet, noisy. On a large sheet of paper, find a way of representing a house with many rooms. Provide an open door and picture of Jesus holding the door open. Stick the pin or stick figures onto the rest of the paper as a crowd going towards the house. Use a speech bubble to show Jesus saying the words, ' In my Father's house are many rooms. I am going there to prepare a place for you . . . I am the way and the truth and the life.' Talk then about ways in which Jesus is 'the way and the truth and the life.'

- Read the Gospel passage together and then imagine a conversation that might have taken place between Thomas and Philip after the resurrection as they looked back together and remembered what they had said to Jesus before the crucifixion. In a small booklet, write down some of the reactions you think they could have had and make this part of the fifth station or page of *Experiences of the Resurrection*. Add also to the presentation the words 'Believe me when I say that I am in the Father and the Father is in me. I tell you the truth, anyone who has faith in me will do what I have been doing.' Add pictures or written accounts of actions which have been inspired by people knowing Jesus.

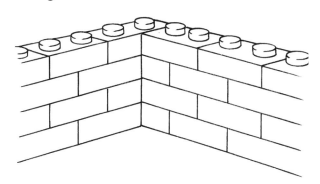

 ## Prayers/ intercessions

Either give everyone a stone and a square of paper as they come into church, or build a wall of bricks, or draw a brick wall on a large piece of paper and place it somewhere accessible in the church.

During the prayer time invite people to write prayers they wish to offer on the pieces of paper. Either these may be stuck on the wall or people could be invited to build their stones into a wall and place the prayer papers at the bottom of the wall. At the beginning and

end of the prayers, a leader may use the sentence 'See, I lay a stone in Zion, a chosen and precious cornerstone, and the one who trusts in him will never be put to shame.'

During the writing and placing of the prayers you could sing either 'O Lord hear my prayer' or 'Be still and know that I am God'.

 ## Stories and other resources

Michelle Magorian, *Goodnight Mr Tom*, Puffin, 1981 (the final chapter)

The Complete Children's Liturgy Book, (p. 56)

Mary Joslin, *Miracle Maker*, Lion, 1998

 ## Drama

'Celebration', in *Livewires Live* (p. 87)

 ## Music

Be still and know that I am God (HON 52, SHF 37)

Christ is our cornerstone (HAMNS 161, HON 77, HTC 564)

Let your restless hearts be still (WGS 2, p. 36)

O Lord, hear my prayer (HON 379, MT 2 p. 56)

Thou art the way, by thee alone (HAMNS 128, HON 512, HTC 113)

We are being built into a temple (SHF 567)

When from the sky in the splendour of summer (CP 132)

We could also suggest listening to a recording of 'Come my way, my truth, my life' (The Call) from Vaughan Williams, *Five Mystical Songs*, words by George Herbert.

Post communion prayer

Eternal God,
whose Son Jesus Christ is the way, the truth and the life:
grant us to walk in his way,
to rejoice in his truth,
and to share his risen life;
who is alive and reigns, now and for ever.

The Sixth Sunday of Easter

 ## Readings

Genesis 8.20 – 9.17

The Lord promises that he will never again destroy all living creatures as he has done. He sends a rainbow as a sign of his covenant with the earth.

Acts 17.22-31

Paul's travels bring him to Athens where he meets with the city council on the Areopagus (Mars' Hill), near the Acropolis and at the centre of city life. Paul skilfully marries his knowledge of Greek philosophy with his knowledge of Jewish teaching, and his newly found faith in the risen Jesus, to commend this faith to the Athenians.

1 Peter 3.13-22

It is possible that at the time this was written, Christians were already beginning to suffer persecution for their faith. The writer commends gentle confidence to the readers. It is better, as Christ did, to suffer for doing good than for doing evil.

John 14.15-21

This passage is a continuation of Jesus' teaching at the Last Supper. Anticipating the trials that they will face in the future, he speaks of a Counsellor who will be with them through it all. Those who know Jesus will not be alone; those who have given him their love will know God's love.

Collect

God our redeemer,
you have delivered us from the power of darkness
and brought us into the kingdom of your Son:
grant, that as by his death he has recalled us to
   life,
so by his continual presence in us he may raise us
   to eternal joy;
through Jesus Christ your Son our Lord,
who is alive and reigns with you,
in the unity of the Holy Spirit,
one God, now and for ever.

 ## Talk/address/ sermon

What is faith? You could invite people to contribute words to form a list on a flip chart. It is almost impossible to arrive at a precise definition. As we pass through the time between Lent and Pentecost, we witness the roller-coaster ride of faith of Jesus' disciples. (You could illustrate this with a picture of a roller-coaster, writing on the coaches the 'low' and 'high' experiences.) He warns them he will leave them, he is tried and killed and they are both sad and terrified. He is risen and appears to them from time to time, restoring their confidence but never stopping long. He promises a new baptism – with the Holy Spirit – and then he is gone, the departure witnessed by his most faithful friends. Today's readings show some of the different aspects of the kind of faith that carries people through the ups and downs of the Christian life. Paul, in speaking to the Athenians, has to think and craft his words carefully. Peter knows it will be necessary to suffer, and there will be fear, but also that we have the assurance of Christ through all. Above all, Jesus says that if we love him, we will obey him and will know the assurance of his presence. Over the last few weeks, as we do every year at this time, we have travelled the roller-coaster with the disciples. The next days mark the end of the journey, at the top of the curve as the Holy Spirit comes and the possibilities of the world of faith are displayed before us.

Congregational/ group activities

- Find out where Athens is and something about the beliefs and philosophies of the Athenians. Many children will have some knowledge about this from work on the Ancient Greeks undertaken in school history projects. School resources on the Greeks will, in any case, be a good source for this information. Ask everyone to sit down and imagine they are the 'Men of Athens'. Ask one person to read out Paul's speech recorded in the reading from Acts (or an edited version if you judge the reading to be too long). Then ask the 'Men of Athens' to talk about Paul's speech. Are they going to be among those who 'became followers of Paul' and if so what convinced them?

- Talk about what an orphan is. Imagine what it would feel like to be an orphan and how you might be comforted. Try to identify some places in the world where being an orphan is still a relatively frequent experience and use the literature published by mission organizations and charities to see how this affects children's lives. Note too how children who are orphans are being offered love and care. Perhaps you could make a poster about this to put in the church. Then talk about what comfort the disciples would want when Jesus left them.

- Make the sixth station or page of *Experiences of the Resurrection*. Think back over the previous five weeks – or indeed look at the experiences recorded over the last five weeks in this exercise. Then make a list of what people have come to know and understand about God (and about Jesus) over these five weeks. Cut up the statements and make them into little flags. Then cut out some people: you can either draw stick people or you may prefer to cut out pictures of anonymous individuals from newspapers or magazines. Give each of the flags to one of the cut-out figures and fix them into the station or onto the page. Add the words from the Gospel reading 'But you know him, for he lives with you and will be in you.'

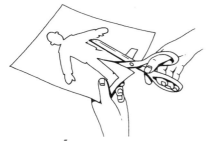

Prayers/ intercessions

Pray for the coming of the Spirit and use this response, based on words from the Gospel, for the prayers.

Leader Jesus said, 'Because I live, you also will live'.

All **Lord, you are in me, and I am in you.**

Pray for the Church and ourselves as Christ's witnesses; for confidence in the proclamation of the Gospel and wisdom to share it appropriately in whatever circumstances we find ourselves.

Pray for those in authority and those in a position to influence public opinion. Pray for ourselves; for the courage to act in accordance with our conscience.

Pray for those who are in need; for orphans and organizations which offer care and compassion, for all who are lonely and alone. Pray that we would be increasingly open to their needs.

Give thanks for the resurrection of Jesus Christ, who has gone into heaven and is at God's right hand. Give thanks for the hope it gives to all who die in the faith of Christ.

Stories and other resources

C.S. Lewis, *The Last Battle*, (Chapter 16, 'Farewell to Shadowlands'), Puffin, 1956

'From Philippi to Athens' (Acts 17), in *The Dorling Kindersley Illustrated Family Bible* (p. 348)

Pat Wynnejones, *The Tale of Geronimo Grub*, Lion, 1990

Ann Holm, *I am David* (The final part of the final chapter starting at 'David stood in the big city and looked around him'.), Magnet, 1965

'A Goose called Gloria' by Jean Watson, in Pat Alexander, *Song of the Morning, Easter Stories and Poems for Children*, Lion, 1997

The Complete Children's Liturgy Book (p. 56)

'Witnesses', in *Pick and Mix* (p. 174)

Drama

'The Son of God', in *Livewires Live* (p. 105)

Music

All over the world the Spirit is moving (HON 16)

Come down O Love Divine (HAMNS 156, HON 90, HTC 231)

Dear Lord and Father of mankind (HAMNS 115, HON 106, HTC 356, SHF 76)

God has put a circle round us (BBP 46)

God of mercy, God of grace (HAMNS 179, HON 175, HTC 293)

Love will never come to an end (CP 99)

Our blest redeemer (HAMNS 151, HON 410)

Spirit of peace, come to our waiting world (CP 85)

Ubi Caritas (HON 525)

Post communion prayer

God our Father,
whose Son Jesus Christ gives the water of eternal life:
may we thirst for you,
the spring of life and source of goodness,
through him who is alive and reigns, now and for ever.

The Seventh Sunday of Easter

Sunday after Ascension Day

 ### Readings

Ezekiel 36.24-28

The Lord tells the Israelites that he will cleanse them and give them a new spirit. They will keep his laws and live in the God-given land of their ancestors.

Acts 1.6-14

Before his ascension Jesus promises the disciples the gift of the Holy Spirit. This will be an endowment of power to enable them to serve their Lord and fulfil his will. Jesus' ascension is an important part of his ministry. If he had not returned to his Father in heaven, he could not have sent the Holy Spirit. The disciples obey their Lord's commandment by returning to Jerusalem where they wait for the gift and meet together for worship.

1 Peter 4.12-14; 5.6-11

Those who are living their lives according to Christ's commands can expect suffering and persecution for his sake. Peter encourages his readers to be alert and to stand firm.

John 17.1-11

In the presence of his disciples Jesus speaks to his Father in heaven. He speaks of the completion of his work on earth according to his Father's will. He has made his Father known to the people he has met. Jesus prays for the disciples that they may know God's protecting presence and the unity which that brings.

Collect

O God the king of Glory,
you have exalted your only Son Jesus Christ
with great triumph to your kingdom in heaven:
we beseech you, leave us not comfortless,
but send your Holy Spirit to strengthen us
and exalt us to the place
   where our Saviour Christ is gone before,
who is alive and reigns with you,
in the unity of the Holy Spirit,
one God, now and for ever.

 ### Talk/address/ sermon

Obedience and waiting

Between Ascension and Pentecost there is a period of waiting on God. The disciples were obedient in this uncertainty and in the unknown. They were told to return to the city (they did!), to wait (they did!) and, as they waited, they worshipped and experienced fellowship. A model for discipleship for today.

Reliance on God

Jesus promises the gift of the Holy Spirit. He makes it clear that the disciples need it. He does not expect them to live and work without it. How often we try to work in our own strength. Peter warns of the suffering we must expect and our own strength is not adequate. God's Holy Spirit is there to equip us for these trials.

The protection and blessing of God

Jesus' prayer for his disciples must be his prayer for us too.

 ### Congregational/ group activities

* Before the service wrap boxes attractively to look like presents. Attach a label to each of the wrapped boxes bearing one of the names of the

gifts and the fruits of the Spirit. Put all the labelled, wrapped boxes in a large, attractively wrapped large container. To this outer box attach a label 'WAIT: not to be opened until next Sunday!' Use this to build up a sense of anticipation/obedience/waiting.

- On a sheet of paper draw four concentric circles and label each one of them with the areas in which the disciples were called to witness. Photocopy this sheet so that there is one for each person in the congregation. Ask them to identify *their* Jerusalem (where I am), *their* Judaea (a bit further away), their Samaria etc. Use these details in the intercessions.

- Develop the idea that Jesus had to leave his earthly life, restricted by time and locality, in order to return to heaven to be there for everyone. Have a large display board at a focal point in church with the heading 'Jesus is for Everyone'. Give out small paper circles on which people draw themselves and write their name. This personalized circle is stuck to the display thus helping everyone to feel embraced by the love of Jesus.

Prayers/ intercessions

Jesus said: *'you will be my witnesses in Jerusalem, in all Judaea and Samaria, and to the ends of the earth.'*

Lord God we bring to you the 'Jerusalem' of our lives. We think of the places where we live and work – the context of our daily lives especially . . .

Lord help us to use the opportunities you give us.

Lord God we bring to you the 'Judaea' of our lives. We think of those situations in which we are involved a bit further away from home. We pray for the needs of our town and region especially . . .

Lord help us to use the opportunities you give us.

Lord God, we bring to you the 'Samaria' of our lives as we pray for our country and all who govern her.

Lord, help Christian people throughout the land to use the opportunities you give us.

Lord God we pray for the World . . . especially . . .

Lord, help Christian people throughout the world to use the opportunities you give us.

Lord open our ears to the needs of others.

Open our hearts so that we can freely give of your love both near and far.

For the sake of Jesus Christ who gave Himself to save the world. Amen.

Stories and other resources

'No fleas, no bugs' (Story 27 – a story about the work of Gladys Aylward and Jeannie Lawson telling in an amusing way how they responded to Jesus' command to go to the uttermost parts of the Earth), in *50 Five Minute Stories*

'Ascension' (chapter 25), in *Children Celebrate!*

'God's amazing humility' (p. 21), 'Christ in glory' (p. 22), 'Citizens of heaven' (p. 45), in *Things to Do in Young People's Worship*

'Ascension', in *Pick and Mix* (pp. 10–14)

 ## Drama

'Not the end', in *Plays for All Seasons*

 ## Music

Come and praise the Lord our King (JP 34)

Crown him with many crowns (HAMNS 147, HON 103, HTC 174, SHF 75)

Everyone matters to Jesus (JU p. 2)

Go tell it on the mountain (HON 165)

He is Lord (HON 204, HTC S.7, JP 139, JU p. 92)

Jesus' love is very wonderful (JU p. 14)

Lord, enthroned in heavenly splendour (HAMNS 263, HON 309, HTC 416, SHF 336)

Rejoice! the Lord is king (HAMNS 139, HON 432, HTC 180, SHF 463)

Post Communion Prayer

Eternal God, giver of love and power,
your Son Jesus Christ has sent us into all the world
to preach the gospel of his kingdom:
confirm us in this mission,
and help us to live the good news we proclaim;
through Jesus Christ our Lord.

Day of Pentecost

Whit Sunday

 ## Readings

Acts 2.1-21

Jesus' promise of the gift of the Holy Spirit is fulfilled. On the day of Pentecost the disciples are filled with the Holy Spirit and begin to speak in other languages. Jews from other nations, gathered in Jerusalem for Pentecost, hear the disciples speaking in languages which they can understand. Bystanders mistake this manifestation of the Spirit for drunkenness but Peter disputes this in a powerful message.

or

Numbers 11.24-30

The Spirit of the Lord rests on the gathered elders of the people and several begin to prophesy. Joshua wants this to be stopped, but Moses encourages them with the words, 'Would that all the Lord's people were prophets, and that the Lord would put his spirit on them!'

1 Corinthians 12.3b-13

These verses list the gifts given to different people by God's Holy Spirit. The gifts we receive vary and the work which they enable us to do varies accordingly, but for all the differences their source is the same – the Holy Spirit. It is this same Spirit which draws together Jew and Gentile, slave and free in a unity which He alone can give.

John 20.19-23

Jesus appears to his disciples, gathered behind locked doors in an upper room soon after his resurrection. He prays for them in the words 'Peace be with you' and 'Receive the Holy Spirit'. He links the enabling power of the Holy Spirit to experiencing and exercising forgiveness.

or

John 7.37-39

Jesus gives the clear call to all who will hear, that any who are thirsty should come to him and drink. For as Scripture says 'Out of the believer's heart shall flow rivers of living water'.

Collect

God, who as at this time
taught the hearts of your faithful people
by sending to them the light of your Holy Spirit:
grant us by the same Spirit
to have a right judgement in all things
and evermore to rejoice in his holy comfort;
through the merits of Christ Jesus our Saviour,
who is alive and reigns with you,
in the unity of the Holy Spirit,
one God, now and for ever.

 ## Talk/address/ sermon

The verses from Acts are concerned with the universal nature of the working of God's Holy Spirit – it is not limited by language, distance or time. It is all-knowing and all-embracing. This applies to word and action. The Spirit has the power to break down barriers and unify what otherwise can only be divided. Peter's message gives examples of how the gift of the Spirit is for *all*.

Modern examples from Northern Ireland and South Africa etc. give contemporary evidence of the power of God's Spirit to achieve what, in human terms, is impossible.

 ## Congregational/ group activities

• Provide, or make, bunches of streamers to wave during the singing of lively Pentecost hymns and songs. Red, orange and yellow plastic carrier bags cut into ribbons are ideal for this purpose. Use sticky tape to attach bunches of flame coloured ribbons to a strong drinking straw or a short, thin garden cane.

• Plan for people in the congregation who can speak other languages to come prepared to pray the Lord's Prayer (or other suitable prayer) in the language which they can speak. Invite them in church just to say the first line separately so that people hear the different languages but then get everyone praying the prayer together (at the same time). This works well using the words of a short song or chorus, e.g. 'Spirit of the Living God, fall afresh on me'.

- Practise making the sound of the wind with simple home-made percussion instruments (sometimes percussion instruments can be borrowed from a local school). Practise the rise and fall of the wind and changing speeds. Get a group to create a wind dance. This is designed to show that the wind of God's Holy Spirit will go when and where it will and that we must be ready to respond.

- Make simple cardboard badges in the shape of a flame or a dove so that during the course of the service everyone is given one.

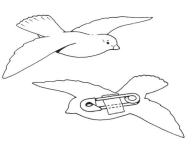

- Involve the children's groups meeting in the week(s) before Pentecost in the making of flame and dove mobiles to hang in church on the day of Pentecost.

- Make a birthday cake. Talk about the Day of Pentecost being the birthday of the church and that on this day (as on any birthday) we celebrate both the birth and the continuing life.

Prayers/ intercessions

Use the following prayer to begin a time of intercessions:

We praise you, O God, because you gave the Holy Spirit to the first Christians, making Jesus real to them, teaching them the truth, giving them power to witness boldly and filling them with his fruit. Grant that in our family love, joy, peace, patience, kindness, goodness, faithfulness, gentleness and self-control may prevail and those around us may take note that we have been with Jesus, your Son. For his sake. **Amen**

Michael Botting (ed.), *Prayers for all the Family*, Kingsway, 1993 (no. 273)

Alternatively, use one of the following prayers:
Confession, *Church Family Worship*, 310
Prayer for God's Spirit, *Church Family Worship*, 324
'Pentecost prayer resources' in *A Church for All Ages* (pp. 212–214)

Stories and other resources

Story 12 ('Empty the bubblewand' – the Fruits of the Spirit) and Story 49 ('The Promise' – the Holy Spirit), in *50 Five Minute Stories*

Leslie Francis and Nicola Slee, *The Windy Day: Teddy Horsley Learns about the Holy Spirit*, NCEC, 1987

'Pentecost' in *Children Celebrate!* (chapter 27)

'Flame of praise' (p. 183) and 'Fruit of the Spirit activity' (p. 190), in *A Church for All Ages*

'Filled with the Spirit', in *100 Talks for All Age Worship* (p. 123)

Susan Sayers, *Things to do in Young People's Worship*, Kevin Mayhew, 1997 (pp. 13, 25, 54)

Drama

Michael Botting (ed.), Drama no. 24 'A farewell present' – Act 1; Drama no. 25 'Holy Spirit – who are you?'; Drama no. 26 'Climbing' (based on 1 Corinthian 12), in *Drama for all the Family*, Kingsway, 1993

'That's the Spirit', in *Plays for all Seasons*

'Prayer is like breathing', in *Acting Up*

'Pentecost rap', *A Fistful of Sketches*

'Pentecost Day', in *Telling Tales*

John Cooper, 'Wine or spirit?', in *Together for Festivals*

Music

Be bold, be strong (JU p. 40)

Come, Holy Ghost, our souls inspire (HAMNS 93, HON 92, HTC 589)

Come thou Holy Spirit, come (HAMNS 92, HON 97, HTC 227)

Give me oil in my lamp (MP 167)

God's not dead! (JU p. 38)

Love, joy, peace and patience (JP 158)

O worship the King all glorious above (HAMNS 101, HON 393, HTC 24, SHF 428)

Spirit of God as strong as the wind (CP 63)

Spirit of God, show me Jesus (MP 609)

Spirit of the living God (HON 455)

Post communion prayer

Faithful God,
who fulfilled the promises of Easter
by sending us your Holy Spirit
and opening to every race and nation
the way of life eternal:
open our lips by your Spirit,
that every tongue may tell of your glory;
through Jesus Christ our Lord.

Day of Pentecost

Trinity Sunday

 ## Readings

Isaiah 40.12-17,27-31

Isaiah offers a string of examples which show the might and incomparable power of God. He is the all-knowing, all-seeing Creator God. However, he is never tired or weary and is always there to strengthen and renew those who turn to him.

2 Corinthians 13.11-13

In the closing words of Paul's second letter to the Corinthians we have an exhortation to godly living and he then uses a trinitarian formula – *'The grace of the Lord Jesus Christ, and the love of God, and the fellowship of the Holy Spirit be with you all'*.

Matthew 28.16-20

Jesus commissions his disciples for their missionary work. He tells them to go to people everywhere, baptizing in the name of Father, Son and Holy Spirit and teaching them obedience. Jesus' words to his disciples end with the utter assurance that he will always be with them, to the end of time.

Collect

Almighty and everlasting God,
you have given us your servants grace,
by the confession of a true faith,
to acknowledge the glory of the eternal Trinity
and in the power of the divine majesty to worship
  the Unity:
keep us steadfast in this faith,
that we may evermore be defended from all
  adversities;
through Jesus Christ your Son our Lord,
who is alive and reigns with you,
in the unity of the Holy Spirit,
one God, now and for ever.

 ## Talk/address/ sermon

Link the theme of the day to the words of the Creed used in the service. The form used at a baptism is very direct and uncluttered in expression

and good for this purpose. What do these statements say about:

God the Father   Jesus the Son   God the Holy Spirit?

What do the readings tell us about:

Creator   Redeemer   Enabler   Comforter?

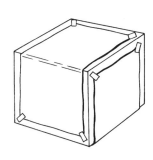

Illustrate and develop this by taking a cube-shaped box (empty) or its equivalent. Cover two adjacent sides with one colour of paper. Cover two adjacent sides with a second colour of paper. Cover the remaining two sides with a third colour of paper. [One box – three colours]

Describe the box when viewed from one angle (red). Repeat with the other two colours. All three descriptions are correct when viewed from a given angle. Use this to help people develop the concept of One God – Three Persons. All can be described differently but are part of the same Godhead.

Congregational/ group activities

- Make three banners/pictures/posters each one representing one of the parts of the Creed (Persons of the Godhead – Father, Son, Holy Spirit). Before the Creed these three visuals are carried to the front of the church. One on the left, one on the right and one in the centre. As the minister asks 'Do you believe and trust in God the Father who made the world' he/she stands beside the appropriate picture. As the second question is asked the minister moves across to stand beside the second picture and likewise the third.

- Divide people into groups of mixed ages and invite them to write their own creed stating *in their own words* what they really believe about Father, Son and Holy Spirit.

- Sing three songs together – one after the other. Choose the songs so that one majors on God as Father, one on Jesus and one on the Holy Spirit. During the singing of these songs some children (and adults?) make a tableau at the front of the church by carrying symbols representative of the words of the songs, in turn representative of the three Persons of the Trinity:

Father:	Symbols of creation and of the wonder and beauty of the world and the universe.
Son:	Cross, chalice, shepherd's crook, lighted candle, etc.
Holy Spirit:	Cut-out flames, dove, fruit shapes with fruit of the Spirit on etc.

Suggested songs could include:

Father:	My God is so big Who put the colours in the rainbow? Stand up, clap hands, shout thank you Lord Father God, I wonder how I managed to exist
Son:	Jesus' love is very wonderful Jesus, name above all names Jesus, how lovely you are
Holy Spirit:	Spirit of the Living God Wind, wind, blow on me All over the world the Spirit is moving.

- Sing 'Father we love you' as someone dances using a long coloured ribbon to wave and weave in the air. This is repeated by another person with a different coloured ribbon for the 'Jesus' verse and a third person with a different coloured ribbon for the 'Holy Spirit' verse. The musicians might play the music for a fourth verse as the congregation hums the tune the three differently coloured ribbons can be intertwined and placed on the altar.

Prayers/ intercessions

Choose three people in advance to lead these prayers. Their parts are marked as A, B and C:

A   Father Almighty, for your majesty and your mercy – loving us still in our waywardness, forgiving us in our unworthiness: we bring you our worship

And offer you thanksgiving.

B   Jesus, our Redeemer, for your humility and your sacrifice – sharing our joys and sorrows, dying and rising for our salvation: we bring you our worship

And offer you thanksgiving.

C   Holy Spirit of God, for your guidance and your encouragement – inspiring and empowering the church, revealing to us all truth: we bring you our worship

And offer you thanksgiving.

God of gods –
Father, Son and Holy Spirit,
Eternal Lord, Three-in-One:

To you be glory, honour and praise,
For ever and ever. Amen.

Michael Perry (ed.), 'Thanksgiving for Trinity Sunday' 13:29, in *Prayers for the People*, Marshall Pickering, 1992

Alternatively, use one of the following prayers:

Michael Perry (ed.), 'Thanksgiving for Trinity Sunday' 13:30, and 13:31, in *Prayers for the People*, Marshall Pickering, 1992

Michael Botting (ed.), 'Simplified Collects' Prayers 53 and 54, in *Prayers for all the Family*, Kingsway, 1993

Stories and other resources

'Trinity', in *Festive Allsorts* (p. 34)

'Trinity' (chapter 27), in *Children Celebrate!*

'Describing God', in *100 Talks for All Age Worship* (p. 12)

Drama

Michael Botting (ed.), Drama no. 28: 'The house with three owners', in *Drama for all the Family*, Kingsway 1993

 ## Music

Father, we adore you (HON 125, SHF 96)

Father we love you (HON 126, SHF 98)

Holy, holy, holy (HAMNS 95, HON 212, HTC 594, SHF 168)

Holy, holy, holy is the Lord (HON 211, SHF 166)

I bind unto myself today (HON 225, HTC 5)

I'm going to shine, shine, shine (JP 392)

Praise God from whom all blessings flow (HON 417, SHF 436)

Sing praise (JP 455)

Three in One and One in Three (HON 515, HTC 12)

Post communion prayer

Almighty and eternal God,
you have revealed yourself as Father, Son and
    Holy Spirit,
and live and reign in the perfect unity of love:
hold us firm in this faith,
that we may know you in all your ways
and evermore rejoice in your eternal glory,
who are three Persons yet one God,
now and for ever.

Sunday between 29 May and 4 June

(if after Trinity Sunday)

Proper 4

 ### Readings:

Continuous

Genesis 6.9-22; 7.24; 8.14-19

Noah is living as a good man in a world of wickedness and violence. He is told by God the exact instructions for building a boat to house his family and two of every kind of living creature. The inhabitants for this boat will survive a mighty flood which comes to destroy God's people. Noah is utterly obedient to God's command. When the waters subside, the people and the creatures leave the boat in order to reproduce and spread over the earth.

or Related

Deuteronomy 11.18-21,26-28

The people of God are urged to follow him and his commandments always. His acts of salvation from Pharaoh and Egypt, and the days in the wilderness are reminders of what their own eyes have seen of his great deeds.

Romans 1.16-17; 3.22b-28,[29-31]

Everyone has sinned and has chosen to turn their back on God. But through the free gift of grace, given to us through God's only Son, Jesus, we can be put right with him. Jesus died for the sins of all. Through his sacrifice we can be forgiven through faith in him. We have not earned this, nor do we deserve it. It is given freely to us through faith alone.

Matthew 7.21-29

Jesus told the parable of the two houses to draw the distinction between those who are hearers and doers of Christ's words and those who are hearers only. The storm in the parable could be the Last Judgement or any time of severe testing. Jesus promises that lives of active obedience will weather the storm and indeed Judgement Day.

 ### Talk/address/ sermon

The story of Noah illustrates the way in which God attempted to give his world a new start through the life of one good man, Noah. This, of course, was to no avail, because of the sinfulness of the human race. He could only really give the world another chance, a new beginning, through the life of one good man, his only son, Jesus.

Link the parable of the two houses to another rabbinical parable 'A man whose knowing exceeds his doing is like a tree with many branches and few roots'. Jesus' teaching is different to all others because he makes all depend upon the doing of his own words. *My words . . . my* design for life is the only one that will last.

Words without action and action without faith are both shallow and not according to God's command – God wants the words and the action rooted in faith in him – it is not an either/or with God but *both*!

 ### Congregational/ group activities

- Give two different children/adults a sack containing all kinds of boxes, cartons, tins etc. and ask them to build the highest structure they can. Obviously they have to choose the biggest and heaviest items for the bottom of the structure. Many children will not do this and their building will collapse. Some adults won't check everything in the sack before they start and, therefore, make unwise choices in the process. The way in which this task is tackled helps discussion about firm foundations and what those are for the Christian.

- Talk about new beginnings. List all the different kinds of new beginnings which people can think of. Identify the different kind of aspirations associated with each new beginning, e.g. new school, new

those who have been betrayed and who are bitter and
    angry

those who have wasted opportunities and who live with
    regret

those who live with failure and debt.

All Help them to find the hope of a new beginning.

**Help them to find the Rock on which to rebuild
their lives.**

**We pray in the name of God's One True Son,
Jesus Christ. Amen**

 ## Stories and other resources

Lionel Fanthorpe, Poems based on the story of Noah,
in *Noah and the Great Flood*, Bishopsgate Press, 1992

All Aboard Noah's Ark, Candle Books, 1997

Linda Parry, *Where is Noah?*, Hunt and Thorpe, 1996

 ## Drama

'Mr Noah and the great flood' (p. 7), 'Noah and the
ark' (p. 8), 'The two houses' (p. 28), in *Telling Tales*
(all-age interactive Bible stories and readings)

 ## Music

Do not be afraid (HON 111)

Don't build your house on the sandy land (JP 39)

God is our strength and refuge (HTC 527)

How firm a foundation (HON 216, HTC 430)

Mister Noah built an ark (JP 167)

Noah was the only good man (JP 432)

Rock of ages (HAMNS 135, HON 437, HTC 444, SHF
469)

The wise man built his house upon the rock (JP 252,
JU p. 50)

Through all the changing scenes of life (HAMNS 209,
HON 516, HTC 46)

uniform, new friends, new opportunities, new languages to learn. What was the new beginning God
offered through Noah and what is the new beginning he still offers through Jesus?

- Display a poster or overhead projector slide which
  reads '*Every Day a New Beginning*'. People could
  be given A5 versions of this to take home as
  reminders of the service and its theme. Discuss
  this slogan in the light of the story of Noah and the
  new beginnings which Jesus can give.

- Build two houses with large construction bricks or
  Lego. Build one on a brick foundation and the
  other on sand. Invite a child to come and knock
  down the house on the sand at the appropriate
  moment in the story.

Prayers/ intercessions

Lord, many people have built their lives on the sand.
Many have known the disaster of a life collapsing when
storms have raged.

We pray especially for . . .
the homeless and destitute
those who have found it necessary to run away from
    home and family

Collect and Post communion prayer

Advent 1998 to Advent 1999	This service is not used this year
Advent 2001 to Advent 2002	First Sunday after Trinity on p. 30
Advent 2004 to Advent 2005	First Sunday after Trinity on p. 30

Sunday between 5 and 11 June

(if after Trinity Sunday)

Proper 5

 ### Readings

Continuous

Genesis 12.1-9

God tells Abram to leave his homeland and his family to go to a land to which God will lead him. God promises Abram, already an old man, the blessing of many descendants. Unlikely as this seemed, Abram is utterly obedient. He sets out with Sarah, his wife, and Lot, his nephew, their slaves and belongings. In Canaan God tells Abram that this country is the one he will give to Abram's descendants. Abram worships God before travelling to the southern part of Canaan.

or Related

Hosea 5.15 – 6.6

The prophet urges the people to return to their God. However, their love is like a morning cloud, or the morning dew, that vanishes early in the day, rather than the steadfast love that the Lord requires.

Romans 4.13-25

Paul looks back to the example of Abraham as a man of faith and not a man of the Law. Abraham believed and hoped in accordance with God's promises even when things seemed hopeless. Abraham's faith did not weaken. He never doubted God's promise. We too are called to live by faith in Jesus, whose death and resurrection can put us right with God.

Matthew 9.9-13,18-26

Jesus calls the tax collector, Matthew, to be one of his disciples. Matthew obeys. When Jesus is eating with Matthew and other tax collectors and outcasts, some Pharisees question the company Jesus is keeping. Jesus assures them that his work is to be a friend to sinners.

A Jewish official comes to tell Jesus that his daughter has died. He asks Jesus to go to lay hands on her so that she may live again. Jesus does as he is asked. On the way a woman who has been ill for twelve years touches the hem of Jesus' garment and she is healed. When Jesus arrives at the Jewish official's house funeral arrangements are under way, but Jesus takes hold of the girl's hand and she is restored to life.

 ### Talk/address/ sermon

These events show faith and hope in action when the world thinks it is hopeless. Abraham had faith in the God of the impossible as did the Jewish official whose daughter had died and the woman who had been ill for twelve years.

Jesus, keeping company with sinners, explains that this is his work. The physically fit do not need a doctor and the sinless do not need Jesus. Link to the outcasts in our world today and in our own culture. Think of those who are victims of prejudice and exclusion. Does the Church sometimes play a part in this? Where do we sit, round the table with Jesus or outside with the Pharisees?

The action of the woman who, in faith, wanted only to touch the hem of Jesus' garment as he passed by: what is an equivalent of that for us – the glimpse of heaven, the revelation, the insight?

Congregational/ group activities

- Play some trust games where one or more people have to depend totally on other group members for their safety and well-being.

  See: Games 7, 19, 54, 31 in Lesley Pinchbeck, *Theme Games*, Scripture Union, 1993

- Draw a large map which can be seen clearly by the congregation. This is to represent symbolically Abram's journey. Mark some random spots on the map. On reaching each of these, when talking through the journey, ask the congregation to offer reasons why Abram and his party should/should not go on. The number of reasons against continuing the journey far outweigh the reasons for doing so. Use this to illustrate the depth of Abram's faith and obedience.

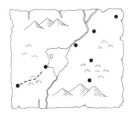

- Have a large sad face on display in church and individual ones photocopied on to card. One is given to each person on arrival in church (6 or 8 can be cut from an A4 sheet). Talk about our sinfulness and the need to repent (sad face). When we have recognized our sin and sought God's forgiveness our lives are changed. Turn the card round. The face that looked so sad is now happy. Jesus is the friend of sinners. He is my/our friend.

- Prepare a mime to accompany the words of the song 'Reach out and touch the Lord as he goes by' (Mission Praise 569). This can also be used line by line as a meditative prayer.

- Make bookmarks or door hangers bearing the words 'You are very special. You are precious in God's sight.' If these are run off on a photocopier time can be given to colouring/decorating them so that they can be taken out to the sick, the elderly, and the housebound after the service.

Prayers/ intercessions

A prayer based on the words of the song 'Reach out and touch the Lord as He goes by' (*Mission Praise* 569)

Reach out and touch the Lord as he goes by . . .
Stop, look, listen, wait . . .
Think of what you want to tell him, ask him (pause)
Reach out now and touch him as he goes by

You'll find he's not too busy to hear your hearts' cry
Don't worry, don't hold back, he's got time for you.
In the rush and the busyness he has time for you,
He can hear you, he can feel you near and
He knows your need

He's passing by this moment your needs to supply
Go on, don't miss this opportunity. He is here.
He knows what you need but tell him

Reach out and touch the Lord as he goes by.
Silence.

Stories and other resources

Michael Botting (ed.), Section 50 'Abraham and the faithfulness of God', in *All in the Family*, Kingsway, 1996

Michael Botting (ed.), Section 74 'Jairus' daughter and the woman who touched Jesus' (a crossword – but based on Luke's account), in *More for all the Family*, Kingsway, 1990

'Jesus and the little girl' (an interactive story), in *Telling Tales*

'Chosen, willing and able' (Abraham), in *100 Talks for All Age Worship* (p. 66)

Lesley and Neil Pinchbeck, *Theme Games*, Scripture Union, 1993

Drama

Cassette tape – Bible Story *Music n' Mime* tape, Side B, Track 10, 'Abraham goes on a journey', Scripture Press, 1991

Music

Abba, Father (HON 5, SHF 1)

Amazing grace (HON 27, SHF 10)

Father Abraham (JU p. 8)

I have a friend   (JP 370)

Immortal Love, for ever full (HAMNS 133, HON 243, HTC 105)

It's hard to say 'I'm sorry' (BBP 75)

Matthew had been sitting (JP 428)

O worship the Lord in the beauty of holiness (HAMNS 49, HON 394, HTC 344, SHF 429)

Reach out and touch the Lord (MP 569)

The God of Abram praise (HAMNS 331, HON 478, HTC 9)

Collect and Post communion prayer

Advent 1998 to Advent 1999	First Sunday after Trinity on p. 130
Advent 2001 to Advent 2002	Second Sunday after Trinity on p. 130
Advent 2004 to Advent 2005	

Sunday between 12 and 18 June

(if after Trinity Sunday)

Proper 6

 ### Readings

Continuous

Genesis 18.1-15 [21.1-7]

Abraham offers hospitality to three travellers. As they eat together one of the men tells Abraham that in nine months' time his wife Sarah will bear a son. Sarah overhears this and laughs because she is past her child-bearing years. God confirms the message by asking 'Is anything too hard for the Lord?' The baby boy is born to Sarah and Abraham in their old age.

or Related

Exodus 19.2-8a

The Israelites journey into the wilderness of Sinai. The Lord speaks to Moses and promises that, if his people follow his commandments, they shall be his treasured possessions above all other people.

Romans 5.1-8

Through faith our relationship with God has been restored and that brings peace. Paul reflects on what this experience of God's grace means. He speaks of testing, endurance and hope. God loves his people so much that he sent his Son to die for them (us) while they (we) are sinners.

Matthew 9.35 – 10.8 [9-23]

Jesus travels around preaching and healing. He feels pity for the crowds of people who seem worried and helpless. He prays to God for workers to be sent out to minister to people in their need. Jesus commissions his twelve disciples to go out to the people of Israel to preach and heal.

 ### Talk/address/ sermon

'Is anything too hard for the Lord?' At first things seem impossible when assessed against human criteria but God has his own ways and it is indeed a lack of our faith if we limit our vision to what God can do by what we consider to be humanly possible.

When Jesus sends out his disciples he is not promising that everything will be easy for them. He anticipates different reactions they will encounter and difficulties they will face and suggests ways of dealing with these. Paul, in his letter to the Romans, speaks of problems associated with discipleship. God only asks for our obedience and not instant success.

'When you come to a town or village, go in and look for someone who is willing to welcome you.' Unpack the implications of this for the Church's work in the community. Link with school, workplace, recreational activities etc. How do we find our starting point for witness and outreach?

 ### Congregational/ group activities

- 'Send us out in the power of your Spirit . . .' Use this prayer from Rite A Eucharist at the end of any service. Invite people to turn around and face the door as they say this prayer so that they look towards the community into which they are being sent. Follow it with words of blessing and dismissal with people still facing the outside.

- Display a large map of the local community. Clearly mark the church building and discuss 'Send us out in the power of your Spirit' in relation to the map. Mark on the map the places to which people are sent in the name of the Church. Use the identified places in the intercessions.

- Draw the shape of a footprint on A4 paper. Carefully print on it the prayer 'Send us out . . .'

Reduce this to appropriate size (4 to an A4 sheet?). Photocopy and give one to each person as they leave church.

- Identify different parts of the church as possible types of places/situations in which we are called to witness. Lay trails of footprints to these places. In the service send people out to these different parts of the building. This could be linked with the prayers. Different parts of the prayer could be led from the different directions.

- Carry a large cross (like ones used in a Good Friday procession) to stand near to where the New Testament reading is being read. Have a silence after the reading. As the cross is carried away someone repeats Romans 5.8.

Prayers/ intercessions

Send us out in the power of your Spirit
– to our schools. We pray especially for . . .
Lord in your mercy, **Hear our prayer.**

Send us out in the power of your Spirit
– to our places of work. We pray especially for . . .
Lord in your mercy, **Hear our prayer.**

Send us out in the power of your Spirit
– to the elderly and housebound. We pray for . . .
– to the sick. We pray for . . .
– to the . . . (identify local needs)
Lord in your mercy, **Hear our prayer.**

Lord we pray that you will send us out in the power of your Spirit to all the people, places and situations which lie ahead in the coming week. We ask for your help so that we may truly live and work to your praise and glory. **Amen**

'About our witness', in Church Family Worship 431

Stories and other resources

'Witness', in Pick and Mix (pp. 174–177)

'Jesus' friends', in Building New Bridges (p. 81)

'Mama Njina's gift' (a story from Kenya based on Romans 5.6-8), in 50 Five Minute Stories

Michael Botting (ed.), 'The people for whom Christ died' (cf. Romans 5.6-11), in For all the Family, Kingsway, 1984

Lesley and Neil Pinchbeck, Games which could be adapted for group use, in Theme Games, Scripture Union, 1993:

Theme point of evangelism: Games 45, 81, 82, 107.

Theme point of fishers of men: Games 48, 51, 76.

Theme point of witnesses and witnessing: Games 130, 50, 82

Drama

'Gifts', in Playing Up

 ## Music

All praise to thee, for thou, O King divine (HAMNS 337, HON 18, HTC 204)

Colours of day (HON 87)

Come on let's get up and go (JP 31)

Everyone matters to Jesus (JU p. 2)

Forth in the peace of Christ we go (HAMNS 458, HON 142, HTC 542)

God's Spirit is in my heart (SLW 93)

Go forth and tell (HON 164)

Send me out from here (MP 594)

The fields are white (JP 237)

We have a gospel to proclaim (MP 728)

Collect and Post communion prayer

Advent 1998 to Advent 1999	Second Sunday after Trinity on p. 130
Advent 2001 to Advent 2002	Third Sunday after Trinity on p. 131
Advent 2004 to Advent 2005	

Sunday between 19 and 25 June

(if after Trinity Sunday)

Proper 7

Readings

Continuous

Genesis 21.8-21

Hagar and her son Ishmael are very jealous of Sarah and her new baby Isaac. Sarah asks Abraham to send Hagar and Ishmael away and God reminds Abraham that the nation he has promised Abraham will come through Isaac. Abraham sends the two off and they wander in the desert. When Hagar feels that Ishmael is going to die, an angel comes to encourage her that a nation will come out of Ishmael and Hagar sees a well of water to quench their thirst.

or Related

Jeremiah 20.7-13

Jeremiah has been prophesying against a priest of Judah. Jeremiah cries out to God complaining about how speaking God's word brings insults and reproach and even his friends are against him, yet he also acknowledges that God is with him.

Romans 6.1b-11

Through baptism we 'die' to sin and can live a new life free from the power of sin.

Matthew 10.24-39

The disciples are encouraged to be confident in speaking about Jesus but also reminded that it is important to put Jesus first in our lives, before even our families. It is in giving up our lives that we gain them. We should not be afraid though because as God cares for even sparrows, He cares for us even more.

 Talk/address/ sermon

What does it mean to be a disciple today? It is often not easy to 'speak directly about Jesus' today. In what ways can this be done effectively in our society? Discuss the many things we value – where does Jesus come in our priorities? Is God just for Sundays or is He important the rest of the week? How can we lay our lives down to gain them and be assured of God's care and concern?

Congregational/ group activities

- Mixed age-groups could look at case studies of people who have courageously spoken out for their faith (e.g. Polycarp, Martin Luther).

- The congregation could each have an outline of a bird to write their name on and decorate. These could be put in a basket or along a string, giving thanks for the way God knows and loves each part of us.

- Design a quiz of Bible characters who spoke out about Jesus or God e.g. Peter, Paul. This could also be done as a crossword on an OHP.

Prayers/intercessions

In confession we could put things that we value e.g. money, CDs, toys etc. in front of the altar and confess how we often value these things more than God.

Prayers could be said with people looking at themselves in a mirror – the person God cares for.

Dying to self (Anon)

When you are forgotten, or neglected, or purposely set at naught, and you don't sting and hurt with the insult but your heart is joyful being counted worthy to suffer for Christ; that is dying to self?

When your good is evil spoken of, when your wishes are crossed, your advice disregarded, your opinions ridiculed, and you refuse to let anger rise in your heart or even defend yourself, but take all in patient, loving silence; that is dying to self?

When you are content with any food, any offering, any climate, any society, any raiment, any interruption by the will of God; that is dying to self?

When you never care to refer to yourself in conversation or record your own good works, or itch after commendations, when you can truly love to be unknown; that is dying to self?

When you see your brother or sister prosper and have his or her needs met and can honestly rejoice with him or her in spirit and feel no envy nor question God, while your own needs are far greater and in desperate circumstances; that is dying to self?

When you can receive correction and reproof from one of less stature than yourself, and can humbly submit inwardly as well as outwardly, finding no rebellion or resentment rising up within your heart; that is dying to self? Are you dead yet?

Stories and other resources

'Polycarp', in *50 Five Minute Stories*

Meryl Doney, *The Very Worried Sparrow*, Lion, 1993

'Trusting in God – Prayer in response', in *One Hundred and One ideas for Creative Prayers*

Virginia Ironside, *The Huge Bag of Worries*, Macdonald Young Books, 1996

Nicola and Stuart Currie, the sections on Janani Luwum and Oscar Romero, in *Seasons and Saints for the Christian Year,* NS/CHP, 1998

Drama

'Careless talk', in *A Fistful of Sketches*

Music

Bread of the world in mercy broken (HAMNS 270, HON 68, HTC 396)

Come, ye faithful, raise the anthem (HAMNS 145, HON 99, HTC 205)

Don't be afraid, (Bible stories with a sung response, CAYP 72)

Everyone matters to Jesus (JU p. 2)

God cares for these (JU p. 56)

How great is our God (JP 82)

There are Hundreds of Sparrows (*Children's Hymn Book*, Kevin Mayhew, 1997, No. 202)

Look and learn from the birds of the air (WP 48)

O for a heart to praise my God (HAMNS 230, HON 361, HTC 483)

Seek ye first (HON 442, SHF 471)

Who put the colours in the rainbow? (JP 288)

Collect and Post communion prayer

Advent 1998 to Advent 1999	Third Sunday after Trinity on p. 131
Advent 2001 to Advent 2002	Fourth Sunday after Trinity on p. 131
Advent 2004 to Advent 2005	

Sunday between 26 June and 2 July

Proper 8

 ## Readings

Continuous

Genesis 22.1-14

God tells Abraham to go and sacrifice his only son. When Abraham was an old man God told him he would have a son, Isaac, who is very precious to Abraham. However, Abraham is obedient and goes to the place of sacrifice, builds an altar and ties Isaac on it. Just as he is about to kill Isaac, an angel speaks to him and praises him that he is even willing to give his beloved son back to God. Just then, Abraham sees a ram caught in the bushes and sacrifices it instead.

or Related

Jeremiah 28.5-9

The prophet Hananiah had prophesied that the oppression from Babylon would end and the holy things that had been taken from the temple would be returned and the exiles could also come back to Judah. Jeremiah asks God to fulfil Hananiah's prophecy. He also says that many prophets speak of disasters but the prophet who speaks of peace, as Hananiah has done, is sent from the Lord if what he prophesies turns out to be true.

Romans 6.12-23

Our whole body is holy and should belong to God and therefore we should not sin. We can choose whether we are sinful, which leads to death, or obedient, which leads to life. Humanly, we are weak, but God can set us free from sin and bring us to eternal life.

Matthew 10.40-42

Jesus says that anyone who welcomes a follower of him, welcomes him and will be rewarded.

 ## Talk/address/sermon

The theme of the Genesis reading is trust. Not blind trust, for Abraham believed God to be merciful and submitted to the test. Through the testing, Abraham is found to have worth and is valued by God. The root of the word 'sin' is an archery term – meaning to fall short. When we sin we fall short of God's expectation of our worth and we become separated from him. Through God's love and through Jesus we can be forgiven and begin again. So we welcome Jesus into our lives as our Redeemer and Reconciler with God. This is the Good News of the Gospels. We are bidden to share this with everyone.

 ## Congregational/group activities

- Show OHP slides/newspaper cuttings of recent events. Ask the groups to talk about where Jesus is in these situations. What should be our response to these? Use the situations and responses as a focus for intercession.

- Groups look up different references (e.g. Mark 9.37, Luke 9.48, 10.16, John 13.20) of people who can be welcomed in Jesus' name. How does this happen in our Church?

- Groups prepare role-plays of ways we can welcome people into God's family today (such as welcoming them into church, visiting them at home, or inviting them for a meal).

- Make invitation cards for special services and church events for friends and neighbours.

- Act out a mime to accompany the song 'When I needed a neighbour, were you there?'

Prayers/ intercessions

For the ugly, the beautiful, those who are 'different', the bully: **we welcome you**.

The bedridden, the elderly, those in hospital, the new born baby: **we welcome you.**

The poor, the homeless, the weak, the hungry: **we welcome you.**

Rune of Hospitality

Leader   Let us stand and say together the words of a Celtic rune of hospitality:

All   **we saw a stranger yesterday,**
we put food in the eating place,
drink in the drinking place,
music in the listening place and,
with the sacred name of the triune god,
he blessed us and our house,
our cattle and our dear ones.

Leader   As the lark says in her song:

Often, often, often, goes Christ in the stranger's guise.

Stories and other resources

'How we belong to God', in *Children and Holy Communion* (p. 31)

Leslie Francis and Nicola Slee, *Teddy Horsley: Neighbours*, NCEC, 1996

Drama

'A new experience', in *Eh Jesus . . . Yes Peter?*, Wild Goose Publications, 1987

Music

All that I am (HON 19)

And now, O Father, mindful of the love (HAMNS 260, HON 32, HTC 392)

Come, Lord Jesus, Come (BBP 29, JU p. 88)

God moves in a mysterious way (HAMNS 112, HON 173, SHF 135)

When I needed a neighbour (HON 548)

Will you come and follow me (HON 560)

Ye servants of God, your Master proclaim (HAMNS 149, HON 565, HTC 520, SHF 628)

Collect and Post communion prayer

Advent 1998 to Advent 1999	Fourth Sunday after Trinity on p. 131
Advent 2001 to Advent 2002	Fifth Sunday after Trinity on p. 131
Advent 2004 to Advent 2005	

Sunday between 3 and 9 July

Proper 9

 ## Readings

Continuous

Genesis 24.34-38,42-49,58-67

Abraham's servant goes to Mesopotamia to look for a wife for Isaac from the same tribe as Abraham. He prays for success and meets Rebecca at the well. Rebecca goes back with the servant and Isaac takes her as his wife.

or Related

Zechariah 9.9-12

A joyful prophecy taken to refer to Jesus' triumphal entry to Jerusalem riding on a donkey.

Romans 7.15-25a

Paul describes the struggle of doing what you don't want to do and know to be wrong and how hard it is to do the good you want to. In some ways it can seem hopeless but we can be encouraged because Jesus can do it for us.

Matthew 11.16-19,25-30

Jesus says that John did not eat or drink and yet people said he had a demon in him and when Jesus eats and drinks they complain. The Good News of the Gospel is simple and can be understood by everybody. God is revealed through Jesus. Jesus promises rest and help for those who are burdened.

 ## Talk/address/ sermon

Part of our Christian way of life is about making choices. Often what we must do is not obvious and we need great courage and support from others, especially if we feel we have failed.

There are many tensions and demands in life and we can easily feel overburdened. We also live in a society that encourages many different values from Christian ones. The readings talk of the way Jesus stands with us to help and strengthen us. We need to be strong in our faith and in what we believe.

 ## Congregational/ group activities

- Bring a very sturdy rope to church and place several mats on the floor (to ensure people have a soft landing in this game!). Divide the children or the congregation into two teams and play a game of Tug of War. This is to illustrate the way that the demands of the world can pull us this way and that.

- 'Temptations': what is right or wrong? Give each group a sheet of paper with a series of temptations written on them. These might include sentences such as 'Driving through a red light', 'Telling a lie', 'Giving back money if over-charged'. Ask them to circle the ones that are particularly strong temptations and add any others that they feel. Stress that no-one else will be shown these pieces of paper.

- Light and Dark: make lists of things that are of the light and those that are of the dark in our lives. These can be used as a basis for intercessions.

- Many Christians have found the words of Matthew 11.28 to be a great comfort, particularly in times of suffering. Prepare a banner or poster with the words: 'Come to me, all you who are weary and burdened, and I will give you rest.' Use some of the ideas in books such as *Banners with Pizazz* (see the Stories and Other Resources section) in planning and creating your banner.

Prayers/intercessions

Place the banner/poster that was created earlier in front of the altar. Ask the congregation to come to the front and place their folded temptations into a container beside the banner. At the end of the prayers, light a candle, saying: 'Jesus said, "Come to me all you who are weary and burdened, and I will give you rest". We place before him these burdens that have weighed us down.' Use the candle to set the pieces of paper alight and ensure they are completely destroyed.

Alternatively, people could be given card bag-shapes to

write a 'burden' on. These can be collected and put on the altar (whilst music is played). Matthew 11.28-30 can be read again.

Pray for those in need, using the following prayer:

Holy God, three in one, we lift to you those in need,
The hungry, the homeless, the helpless,
The sick, the silly, the sad,
The disabled, the disturbed, the deceived,
The anxious, the abused, the addicted,
The imprisoned, the ignored, the isolated,
Holy God, three in one, hear our prayer for those in
    need.
Amen

A Church for All Ages (p. 169)

Stories and other resources

No.3, in *50 Five Minute Stories*

Diane Guelzow, *Banners with Pizazz*, Resource Publications Inc., 1992

Leslie Francis and Nicola Slee, *Teddy Horsley: Night Time*, NCEC, 1996

Drama

'Give and take', in *Scenes and Wonders*

Music

Be bold, be strong (JP 14)

Father lead me day by day (JP 43)

Jesus, lover of my soul (HAMNS 123, HON 261, HTC 438)

Just as I am, without one plea (HAMNS 246, HON 287, HTC 440, SHF 304)

Meekness and majesty (HON 335)

Oh! Oh! Oh! How good is the Lord (HON 397)

Put your hand in the hand (JP 206)

What a friend we have in Jesus (HON 541, HTC 373, SHF 598)

Collect and Post communion prayer

Advent 1998 to Advent 1999	Fifth Sunday after Trinity on p. 131
Advent 2001 to Advent 2002	Sixth Sunday after Trinity on p. 132
Advent 2004 to Advent 2005	

Sunday between 3 and 9 July

Sunday between 10 and 16 July

Proper 10

 ### Readings

Continuous

Genesis 25.19-24

After some years Rebecca becomes pregnant with twins. Esau, the eldest, becomes a hunter and his father's favourite, while Jacob is his mother's favourite. Esau, when he is very hungry, sells his rights as a first-born son to Jacob in exchange for some soup.

or Related

Isaiah 55.10-13

These verses talk of the power of God's word in that it achieves all God wants it to. God also promises that his people will leave Babylon and even the hills and trees will shout for joy.

Romans 8.1-11

In spite of our weak and sinful human nature, God's Spirit controls us and so we can live in union with Christ and without blame. We have been put right by Christ and the Spirit lives in us to control our sinful nature so we can live in a way that pleases God.

Matthew 13.1-9,18-23

The parable of the sower. Jesus tells us a story about the different things that can happen to a seed when it is scattered. He explains that the seed is like the message of God's kingdom and describes how that message sometimes does not have deep roots or becomes tangled in thorns. God wants the message of Good News to be heard, understood, and to take root and grow in each of us. For this to happen we need to listen with open hearts and minds.

 ### Talk/address/ sermon

Following on from the previous two weeks, the readings continue to focus upon how we can grow in our commitment and faith. How do people hear the Gospel in our society? What different things today act as the birds, weeds or roots in the parable and prevent others from hearing the Good News? How can we make sure that seeds/we grow in good deep soil and that strong plants/Christians develop.

 ### Congregational/ group activities

- Use a dramatic reading of the parable (perhaps from the Dramatized Bible). As part of the drama 'entangle' someone in labels/clothes/things to show how material goods can prevent us growing as Christians.

- Give each group a sheet with information about different kinds of seeds. What does each seed need to grow? Where would it be best to plant them? Plant different kinds of seeds in plant pots. Ensure some are given proper light, watering and care. Deprive others of these basic needs. Compare the growth of the plants over the coming weeks.

- Give each group a set of templates (or photo-copied sheets) showing various baby animals and their parents (such as a foal and horse, lamb and sheep). Ask the groups to colour these in, cut them out and stick them on small pieces of card. Each of these pieces of card should be the same size (about the same as in a pack of cards). Play games of Snap or Memory games with these sets.

Prayers/ intercessions

Plant us in the deep soil of your word.
Help us to grow.
Let your Holy Spirit, like rain, refresh us.
Help us to grow.
There are things in us that are still seedlings.
Help us to grow.
For the things that have grown.
Keep us blossoming and bearing fruit.

Alternatively, use the following prayers that affirm our faith:

Christ's Spirit lives in you:
Our spirit is alive
Because we have been put right with God.

The Spirit of God lives in you:
The Spirit is life for us –
Even though our body dies,
God who raised Christ from the dead
Will also give life to us
Through his Spirit who lives in us. Amen

Bible Prayers for Worship 14.10

Stories and other resources

'Why we belong to God', in *Children and Holy Communion*

Leslie Francis and Nicola Slee, *Teddy Horsley: The Song*, NCEC, 1997

Jan Godfrey, *How does a Flower Grow?*, Tamarind, 1995

Drama

'The sower', in *Telling Tales*

Michael Botting (ed.), 'The jam factory' (retelling of parable of sower), in *Drama for all the Family*, Kingsway, 1993

'Farmer Jack' (pantomime version of parable of the sower), in *Plays for all Seasons*

'The parable of the sower', in *Children Aloud!*

Music

Father of heaven, whose love profound (HAMNS 97, HON 124, HTC 359)

Father of mercies in thy word (HAMNS 167, HTC 247)

Glory to God (HON 161)

Just a tiny seed (BBP 67)

Lord thy word abideth (HAMNS 166, HON 318, HTC 251)

Morning has broken (HON 337)

The springtime come (Feeling Good p. 30)

We plough the fields (HON 534, JP 267)

Collect and Post communion prayer

Advent 1998 to Advent 1999	Sixth Sunday after Trinity on p. 132
Advent 2001 to Advent 2002	Seventh Sunday after Trinity on p. 132
Advent 2004 to Advent 2005	

Sunday between 17 and 23 July

Proper 11

 ## Readings

Continuous

Genesis 28.10-19a

When Jacob, on a journey, stops to rest for a night, he has a dream in which he sees a stairway leading up to heaven, with angels going up and down; God is at the top and tells him that He will give him the land where Jacob is lying and that Jacob will have many descendants.

or Related

Wisdom of Solomon 12.13,16-19

Although the Lord has great strength, he uses this power with great kindness and forbearance towards us. In this way he also teaches his people that they must be kind.

Isaiah 44.6-8

The Lord says that there is no other God like him – he is the first and the last and none can compare to him.

Romans 8.12-25

If we put sin to death and live by the Spirit we can be children of God and call God 'Abba Father'. As children we are also heirs, but that may involve us in suffering. All of creation as well as us, God's children, wait in hope for the full resurrection freedom.

Matthew 13.24-30,36-43

In the parable of the weeds, Jesus tells a story of how God plants good seed (God's children) but the devil comes and plants weeds among them. Jesus says that these should grow together until the harvest (judgement at the end of the age) when the good will be separated from the bad.

Talk/address/ sermon

In the world, Christians live side by side with unbelievers but in the last judgement God will separate believers from unbelievers. Many things surround us and act as weeds preventing us growing as Christians should. How can we strengthen our faith? What are our strengths and weaknesses as a community? We need to reach out to a suffering and needy world. How might we do this more effectively?

 ## Congregational/ group activities

- Seeds that look the same can be very different when they have grown. Ask each group to look at the different seeds that were planted last week. Are there any signs of growth? Try some further experiments by 'planting' mustard cress in different kinds of soil – as well as on blotting paper!

- Play the eggshell game. Place six eggshells in a box. Only one is a whole egg – the others are merely shells. See who can guess which this is.

- Muddle up different pieces of coloured wool. Each group member needs to get a different colour from the tangle. Then these can be plaited and woven together and used to decorate the border of a banner.

- Write simple, trinitarian prayers for use in the intercessions. A workshop on writing such prayers in the Celtic tradition can be found in *The Celtic Resource Book*.

Prayers/ intercessions

Use the prayers that were created during the group/activities time. Alternatively, use the following Celtic prayers:

Come I this day to the Father,
Come I this day to the Son,
Come I to the Holy Spirit powerful;
Come I this day with God,
Come I this day with Christ,
Come I with the Spirit of kindly balm.
God, and Spirit, and Jesus,
From the crown of my head
To the soles of my feet;
Come I with my reputation,
Come I with my testimony,
Come I to Thee, Jesu –
Jesus, shelter me.

Carmina Gadelica

May the strength of God pilot us.
May the power of God preserve us.
May the wisdom of God instruct us.
May the hand of God protect us.
May the way of God direct us.
May the shield of God defend us.
May the host of God guard us
Against the snares of the evil one
And the temptations of the world.
May Christ be with us
Christ above us
Christ in us
Christ before us.
May thy salvation O Lord,
Be always ours
This day and for evermore.
Amen.

St Patrick (5th Century)

Stories and other resources

Building New Bridges (p. 68)

Martin Wallace, *The Celtic Resource Book*, NS/CHP, 1998

Talkabout Take-Home sheets 5 and 6, in *Children and Holy Communion*

Leslie Francis and Nicola Slee, *Teddy Horsley: Neighbours,* NCEC, 1996

Drama

'A nice day', in *Wild Goose Prints No.5*, Wild Goose Publications, 1989

'Jacob's ladder', in *Acting Up*

 ## Music

Abba Father (HON 5, SHF 1)

Blessed assurance (HON 62, SHF 41)

Father God, I wonder (HON 119, SHF 92)

Father we love you (HON 126, SHF 98)

God that madest earth and heaven (HAMNS 12, HON 178)

Great is the Lord (HON 185, SHF 141)

Happy are they, they that love God (HAMNS 176, HON 195, HTC 473)

Who is on the Lord's side? (JP 287)

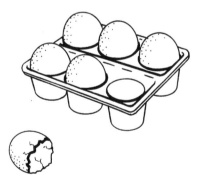

Collect and Post communion prayer

Advent 1998 to Advent 1999	Seventh Sunday after Trinity on p. 132
Advent 2001 to Advent 2002	Eighth Sunday after Trinity on p. 132
Advent 2004 to Advent 2005	

Sunday between 24 and 30 July

Proper 12

 ### Readings

Continuous

Genesis 29.15-28

Jacob stays with his uncle Laban and, in return for seven years' work, wants to marry Laban's younger daughter, Rachel. Laban tricks Jacob and gives him the older daughter and Jacob has to work another seven years for Rachel.

or Related

1 Kings 3.5-12

God appears to Solomon in a dream and asks him for whatever he wants God to give him. Solomon asks for wisdom. God is pleased with this request.

Romans 8.26-39

God's Spirit helps us to pray and prays for us. God works for the good of his children, he chose us, called us, justified us and glorifies us. As God even gave His only Son for us so he will not withhold any good thing from us and nothing can separate us from God or defeat us.

Matthew 13.31-33

Jesus compares the Kingdom of Heaven to a mustard seed and to yeast – small insignificant things that can grow with spectacular results.

 ### Talk/address/ sermon

Use the pots of seeds from the last few weeks' group activities as a visual aid.

God's kingdom starts with small things and grows very large, often in ways that are hard to see or understand. Some things are very small but have great potential. We may seem small, but together we have great potential. We grow and mature not only physically, but mentally and spiritually as well. But each of us is different and all are special in God's eyes.

 ### Congregational/ group activities

- Have a collection of photographs of famous people as children (or members of the church). Can people work out the names of these children?

- Give each person in the group a sheet of paper. Ask them to draw a 'life chart', marking in the important events that have happened to them at different stages of their lives. Children might draw pictures of some sad/happy events that have happened to them.

Ordinary Time (After Trinity)   88

- Collect together different forms of seeds (as colourful as possible). Make seed pictures by gluing these onto coloured card with Matthew 13.31-32 written out in full beneath.

- For this week's guessing game, collect together a number of different seeds in a jar. Ask if people can guess how many different kinds of seed there are and the total number of seeds.

Prayers/ intercessions

Make a collage of the photographs of famous people (or members of the church). Use these as a focus for prayers of thanksgiving and intercession.

Give each person (or group) a large balloon. Ask them to write the name of the person, country or charity they would like to be prayed for. Ask the adults to help the children blow up the balloons. Bring these to the front of the church whilst singing a hymn such as 'Heaven shall not wait'.

Alternatively, use this prayer to dedicate ourselves to God's work:

My talents and my practised skills,
All shall be for you, Lord, all shall be for you,
My gifts and my qualifications,
All shall be for you, Lord, all shall be for you,
The praise for my achievements,
All shall be for you, Lord, all shall be for you,
The credit for my successes,
All shall be for you, Lord, all shall be for you,
The best of my creativity,
All shall be for you, Lord, all shall be for you,
The richness of my imagination,
All shall be for you, Lord, all shall be for you,
The lessons I learn from my failures,
All shall be for you, Lord, all shall be for you,
The whole of my life transformed by your Holy Spirit,
All shall be for you, Lord, all shall be for you.

A Church for All Ages (p. 151)

Stories and other resources

'Kingdom of God', in *Pick and Mix*

Sue Kirby, 'The mustard seed', in *Stories Jesus Told*, CPAS, 1991

David Bell and Terry Clutterham, *Loose the Juice!*, CPAS, 1998

'VIPs – We are all special', in *All Aboard!*

 ## Music

All over the world (HON 16)

Be thou my vision (HAMNS 343, HON 56, HTC 545, SHF 38)

Cry 'Freedom!' (HON 104)

First the seed and then the rain (BBP 51)

God of grace and God of glory (HAMNS 367, HON 174, HTC 324)

Heaven shall not wait (HON 207)

Jesus, priceless treasure (HON 262, HTC 461)

Just a tiny seed (BBP 67)

Collect and Post communion prayer

Advent 1998 to Advent 1999	Eight Sunday after Trinity on p. 132
Advent 2001 to Advent 2002	Ninth Sunday after Trinity on p. 133
Advent 2004 to Advent 2005	

Sunday between 31 July and 6 August

Proper 13

 ## Readings

Continuous

Genesis 32.22-31

Jacob sends his family and everything he has across the stream of Jabbok. During the night a man wrestles with him, putting Jacob's hip out of joint. Jacob insists that the man should bless him, and in doing so the man gives him the name Israel because Jacob had striven with God and humans.

or Related

Isaiah 55.1-5

All those who are in need are told to come to the Lord, for the Lord will make an everlasting covenant with his people.

Romans 9.1-5

Paul tells the Christians in Rome that he speaks the truth in Christ by the working of the Holy Spirit. It is to the Israelites that God made covenants and promises, and from amongst whom the Messiah has come.

Matthew 14.13-21

Some five thousand men, women and children have followed Jesus to the lakeside. It is evening and the disciples want the crowd to go and find food in the villages. Jesus asks the disciples themselves to feed the crowd. Jesus takes and blesses five loaves and two fish which are then given to the crowd. After all have eaten, twelve baskets full of leftovers are collected

 ## Talk/address/ sermon

Jacob had a life-changing encounter which took him on a journey closer to God. Like him, we are called on to a pilgrimage. God brings us from where we are, to where he wants us to be. Those five thousand men, women and children found that God would provide sufficient for our needs. With God, all things are possible. God will never abandon us. What are the ways in which we can say a bigger 'yes' to God? How does your faith in God sustain and feed you in your daily life? What would help in increasing your faith and exploring doubt?

 ## Congregational/ group activities

- Give out pieces of paper cut into fish and loaf shapes, along with pens/crayons/pencils. Ask people to write or draw a picture of some of the gifts and skills God has given them. Collect the fish and loaves in baskets, use these as a sign of what we offer to God to help build his Kingdom.

- Give out paper fish with the words 'All ate and were filled' written on, along with folded sheets of newspaper. With people standing in a line, race the fish to the finishing line using the newspaper to flap the fish along the floor. Talk about following God as a journey, and all who follow him will be given enough for their needs.

- Show two large drawings of suitcases or travel bags. Ask the questions: what do we need to take with us on a long journey? Why are these things important to us? Note the answers on one suitcase. If we are to undertake a pilgrimage to God, what do we need for this journey? Write up answers on the other suitcase.

Prayers/intercessions

Lord God,
We come before you
as your children.
We ask that you will show
our love your way.
Father, in your love:

All   Lead us and feed us.

We pray for:
    those who are on any sort of journey
    members of the family
    all in authority that they may walk by faith
    the sick and suffering, that God's healing grace may
    be poured upon them.
    ourselves as we continue our pilgrimage, remembering those who have gone before us

all ending with the refrain –

Father, in your love
All   Lead us and feed us.

Stories and other resources

Leslie Francis and Nicola Slee, *Teddy Horsley: The Picnic*, NCEC, 1990

'The hungry crowd', *The Puffin Children's Bible*, Puffin Books, 1991

'Jake returns to Canaan', *The Dorling Kindersley Illustrated Family Bible*

'Jesus feeds the crowds', *The Dorling Kindersley Illustrated Family Bible*

'The big picnic', in *Praise, Play and Paint!* (p. 31)

'Food of Belonging' sheet A, in *Children and Holy Communion*

Drama

'Fish and bread' in *Feeling Good!* (dramatic presentation, p. 11)

Music

Bread is blessed and broken (HON 66)

Broken for me, broken for you (HON 72)

Come, Lord, be our guest (WGS 3, p. 102)

Fish and bread (FG p. 11)

Who took fish and bread? (JP 286)

Glorious things of thee are spoken (HAMNS 172, HON 158, HTC 494, SHF 123)

O God, unseen yet ever near (HAMNS 272, HON 367, HTC 421)

Praise to the Lord, the almighty (HAMNS 207, HON 427, HTC 207, SHF 452)

The song of the supper (WGS 2, p. 34)

Collect and Post communion prayer

Advent 1998 to Advent 1999	Ninth Sunday after Trinity on p. 133
Advent 2001 to Advent 2002	Tenth Sunday after Trinity on p. 133
Advent 2004 to Advent 2005	

Sunday between 7 and 13 August

Proper 14

 ### Readings

Continuous

Genesis 37.1-4,12-28

Joseph is a shepherd with his brothers. Their father favours Joseph and gives him a coat of many colours. His brothers plot to kill him, but then decide to sell him to the Ishmaelites for twenty pieces of silver. Joseph is then taken to Egypt.

or Related

1 Kings 19.9-18

Elijah's life has been threatened by Jezebel so he flees into the wilderness. After an angel of the Lord has comforted him, he travels on to a cave on Mount Horeb. The word of the Lord comes to him and tells him to stand on the mountain before the Lord. Here he encounters a great wind, earthquake and fire, before the Lord speaks to him.

Romans 10.5-15

Paul tells the Romans that it is by faith that we are made righteous. By believing with the heart and confessing with our words we are brought closer to God.

Matthew 14.22-33

The disciples go ahead of Jesus by boat to the other side of the lake. Whilst far from the shore the boat begins to be battered by the waves. Jesus walks on the water towards them, making the disciples think he is a ghost. Jesus asks them not to be afraid. Peter walks towards Jesus, and becomes frightened, sinking into the water. Jesus saves Peter, asking why he has so little faith.

 ### Talk/address/ sermon

We have been called to follow God. Sometimes this feels a difficult thing to do; many things press in upon us and sometimes we lose sight of where we are on our faith journey. At times like these we ask God to be there, ready to catch us lest we should fall. We can also share the words in Mark 9 'Lord, I believe; help my unbelief'.

Why did Peter sink?

What helped Peter to walk with Jesus?

What are the ways in which we can keep faith and trust in God?

Who is there to help us if we fall?

 ### Congregational/ group activities

- In pairs, one person is led wearing a blindfold by the other. With great care, lead the person by the hand, asking them sit, walk down steps, turn a corner, negotiate a door.

At the end of this trust exercise, ask those who had been led what it felt like to put their trust in someone else. Ask those who led what it felt like for someone else to have faith in your actions.

Ask the question 'Who helps us to trust in God?'

- On a paper plate draw the person's face who helps you and shows you something about God. If you wish, write their name at the bottom. Place the faces with blu-tack on to the altar frontal as an offering of thanks and praise.

- Make a banner or poster with the title 'Keep The Faith', and include words and pictures on how we can proclaim the word and works of God in our daily lives – at home, at school, at work, in our communities and in our churches.

Prayers/ intercessions

With thanks I pray to you, Lord.
All   With thanks I pray to you.

With praise I pray to you, Lord.
All   With thanks I pray to you.

With hope I pray to you, Lord.
All   With thanks I pray to you.

It's night, I pray to you, Lord.
All   With thanks I pray to you.

It's good, I pray to you, Lord
All   With thanks I pray to you.

It's hard, I pray to you, Lord.
All   With thanks I pray to you.

For trust we pray to you, Lord.
All   With thanks I pray to you.

For health we pray to you, Lord.
All   With thanks I pray to you.

For peace we pray to you, Lord
All   With thanks I pray to you.

'For our spiritual lives',
in *A Church for All Ages* (p.166)

Stories and other resources

'Joseph and his brothers', *The Puffin Children's Bible*

'Joseph and his brothers', and 'Jesus walks on water', *The Dorling Kindersley Illustrated Family Bible*

D. Hilton, 'To Colonel Alexei Leonov' no. 53, in *A Word In Season*, NCEC, 1984

The Word for All-Age Worship, Kevin Mayhew, 1996 (pp. 21 and 75)

'Boiled egg bowling', in *Building New Bridges* (p. 94)

Story and discussion, in *Building New Bridges* (p. 94)

'Colours', in *Under Fives – Alive!* (pp. 74–75)

'Joseph and his brothers', in *More Things To Do In Children's Worship* (p. 60)

'Trusting God', in *More Things To Do In Children's Worship* (p. 37)

 Music

At the name of Jesus (HAMNS 148, HON 46, HTC 172, SHF 26)

Be still and know that I am God (HON 52, SHF 37)

Do not be afraid (HON 111)

Go forth and tell (HON 164, HTC 505)

Jesus is a friend of mine (JP 136)

When the road is rough and steep (JP 279)

With Jesus in the boat (JP 291)

Collect and Post communion prayer

Advent 1998 to Advent 1999	Tenth Sunday after Trinity on p. 133
Advent 2001 to Advent 2002	Eleventh Sunday after Trinity on p. 133
Advent 2004 to Advent 2005	

Sunday between 14 and 20 August

Proper 15

Readings

Continuous

Genesis 45.1-15

Joseph has his brothers brought to him and forgives them. He asks them to bring their father to Egypt so that Joseph may care for him there.

or Related

Isaiah 56.1,6-8

God's people are urged to maintain justice and do what is right, for his salvation will soon come and his deliverance soon be revealed.

Romans 11.1-2a,29-32

Paul tells the Romans that God has not rejected His people. God shows mercy to us even though we may have disobeyed Him.

Matthew 15.[10-20],21-28

A Cananite woman begs Jesus to heal her sick daughter. Through her persistence and seeing her great faith, Jesus heals the woman's daughter.

Talk/address/ sermon

Even though we may not think we deserve it, God's loving forgiveness surrounds us all the time. We are the ones who stop the relationship being put right with God. We are the ones who fail God and fail one another.

What things in our lives do we need to be forgiven for? In what area of our life do we need the love of God the most? What person or situation needs our love and mercy? What are the ways in which we can show God's love and mercy in our daily lives?

Congregational/ group activities

• Place different objects in a bag so that they cannot be seen. Ask different people in turn to place their hand in the bag and guess what one of the objects is. Ask a question about what the object is made of, and if it can change to become something else.

God cannot change to become something he is not; it is not in his nature to be anything other than loving and compassionate.

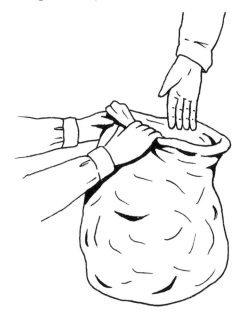

• Ask people in groups to finish the following story:

Jesus and his followers were in the supermarket, buying food for their evening meal. Suddenly, there was a clamour, voices were raised and assistants hurried from various parts of the shop.

A young woman with three small children had been caught shoplifting, the security man was asking her to accompany him to the office and she was refusing. Assistants and customers gathered to watch and to listen. She said it was a mistake, she had been distracted and had not realized what she was doing. The manager spoke out, 'I suppose you were going to pay for it as well, or is that also part of the distraction?'

The woman was silent, she clung to her children and looked down, she began to cry, 'I cannot pay for the things' she said, 'because I haven't any money. I only did it because they are hungry. I'm sorry, please I'm sorry.'

'Sorry won't pay for this food,' said the security man, 'you're a common thief!'

Jesus pushed his way through the crowd, and said . . .

Ask for the groups to share the story ending with the rest of the congregation. Then ask them in what way did Jesus show God's love and mercy? How did we come to make a decision as to what Jesus would say? Are there situations in our life in which the voice of Jesus needs to be heard?

- Give out small pieces of paper and pencils or crayons. Ask people to write or draw something which stops them loving God more fully.

Ask people to come and burn their piece of paper (in a suitable brazier or metal waste bin) as a sign of God's refining love and mercy.

Prayers/ intercessions

Heavenly Father, may this church be full of your love and mercy,

All   That your Kingdom may come.

May our relationships show your kindness and compassion,

All   That your Kingdom may come.

May this nation reflect your love and justice,

All   That your Kingdom may come.

May those who are sick know your healing love,

All   That your Kingdom may come.

As with your Saints, may we shine with your love and life,

All   That your Kingdom may come.

Stories and other resources

'Joseph and his brothers' , *The Puffin Children's Bible*

'Joseph's family in Egypt', *The Dorling Kindersley Illustrated Family Bible*

The Word for All-Age Worship, Kevin Mayhew, 1996 (p. 92)

Drama

'Family reunion', in *Plays For All Seasons* (p. 97)

Music

Among us and before us (WGS 3, p. 104)

A touching place (WGS 3, p. 66)

A woman's care (WGS 1, p. 26)

Forgive our sins as we forgive (HON 141)

God of mercy, God of grace (HAMNS 179, HON 175, HTC 293)

I cannot tell why he whom angels worship (HON 226, HTC 194, SHF 185)

The journey of life (JP 468)

Jesus, Jesus, here I am (JU p. 96)

We cannot measure how you heal (*Love from Below*, Wild Goose Publications, 1989)

We have a gospel to proclaim (HAMNS 431, HON 532, HTC 519)

Collect and Post communion prayer

Advent 1998 to Advent 1999	Eleventh Sunday after Trinity on p. 133
Advent 2001 to Advent 2002	Twelfth Sunday after Trinity on p. 134
Advent 2004 to Advent 2005	

Sunday between 21 and 27 August

Proper 16

 ### Readings

Continuous

Exodus 1.8 – 2.10

The king of Egypt turns his people against the Israelites living there. The Egyptians treat the Israelites harshly and, on the orders of the king, all the newborn boys are to be killed. A couple from the house of Levi give birth to a son whom they place in a basket upon the river. Pharaoh's daughter finds the child and names him Moses.

or Related

Isaiah 51.1-6

All those who seek the Lord are urged to look back to the way the Lord blessed Abraham and Sarah. For the Lord will bring comfort to all the waste places of Zion and bring joy and gladness again.

Romans 12.1-8

Paul tells the Christians in Rome to be a living sacrifice so that they may know the will of God. They are one body in Christ, but each has different gifts according to God's will.

Matthew 16.13-20

In answer to Jesus' question 'Who do you say I am?', Peter tells Jesus that he is the Messiah. Jesus replies by declaring Peter to be the rock on which he will build the church.

 ### Talk/address/ sermon

St Paul tells us that we are one body in Christ, even though we are all different and have many different gifts. Jesus saw that Peter had particular gifts, and announced that it was to be on him that the church was to be built. What qualities and gifts do you think Jesus saw in Peter? What qualities and gifts do you have? What qualities and gifts are necessary to continue to build up the Church? In what way can God shape your life for his service?

 ### Congregational/ group activities

• Give each person a pebble or small stone. Ask people to look at the character and qualities of their rock e.g. is it rough or smooth; what colours does it possess; is it heavy or light? Ask people then to look again at their rock so that it may tell them something about the character of God. How can we reflect these qualities in our lives?

• Give out paper in the shape of a fish, along with pens and crayons. Ask people to write or draw a prayer on the paper, and come and place it in the net which can be hanging in an appropriate place in church (garden netting works well). Pin up large pieces of paper on which there is the outline of a person. Ask people which personal qualities are necessary for the building up of the Church and community. Note the answers on the paper within the outline. This will work well as a small group exercise.

Prayers/ intercessions

Lord, you come among us
as a servant;
not to be served but to serve
Lord,

All Help us give our gifts to you.

Lord, you come to
show people how
to love and to bring the world
back to you
Lord,

All Help us give our gifts to you.

Lord, you healed the sick
and suffering.
We pray for. . .
Lord,

All Help us give our gifts to you.

Lord, you ask us to help
build your kingdom here on earth.
We offer you our lives in your service
Lord,

All Help us give our gifts to you.

Stories and other resources

'Moses hears God's call', in *The Puffin Children's Bible*

'Moses and the Israelites', and 'The Transfiguration', in *The Dorling Kindersley Illustrated Family Bible*

'Gifts', *Pick and Mix* (pp. 68–71)

'Baby Moses', in *Praise, Play and Paint!* (p. 22)

'Moses in the bulrushes', *Under Fives – Alive!* (pp. 18–19)

'Seeing God through people', *More Things To Do In Children's Worship* (p. 10)

'For our gifts', *A Church For All Ages* (p. 127)

Prayers for Children (No. 141)

'Faith has set us on a journey', in *Dare to Dream*, Kevin Mayhew, 1996 (p. 203)

'For lives without prejudice', in *A Church For All Ages* (p. 163)

 ## Drama

Dramatized reading on Baby Moses, *Praise, Play and Paint!* (p. 23)

 ## Music

Bind us together, Lord (HON 60, SHF 39)

Brother, sister, let me serve you (HON 73)

Gifts that last (WGS 3, p. 34)

I love you Lord Jesus (BBP 27)

Jesus is my friend (BBP 78)

Moses, Moses (FG p. 12)

One more step along the road I go (HON 405)

Take my life, and let it be (HAMNS 249, HON 464, HTC 554, SHF 496)

Thou art the Christ, O Lord (HAMNS 317)

We are one family together (*The Children's Hymn Book,* Kevin Mayhew 1997, 219)

Collect and Post communion prayer

Advent 1998 to Advent 1999	Twelfth Sunday after Trinity on p. 134
Advent 2001 to Advent 2002	Thirteenth Sunday after Trinity on p. 134
Advent 2004 to Advent 2005	

Sunday between 28 August and 3 September

Proper 17

 ### Readings

Continuous

Exodus 3.1-15

Whilst Moses is tending sheep, the angel of God appears to him in a flame of fire out of a bush. God speaks and tells Moses that he hears the cries of his people and has come to take them from Egypt into the promised land.

or Related

Jeremiah 15.15-21

The prophet remembers how he was called by God and set apart from others. Jeremiah complains to the Lord about his mistreatment. The Lord promises that the prophet will become like a fortified wall of bronze to his people and that he will be saved and delivered from the hand of the wicked.

Romans 12.9-21

Paul tells the Christians in Rome to live out God's love by serving others. They should be joyful in hope, faithful in prayer and share with all God's people who are in need.

Matthew 16.21-28

Jesus tells his disciples that he is to suffer, to die, and to be raised. At this, Peter declares that this must never happen. Jesus rebukes Peter and tells his disciples that they must take up their cross and follow him, for to save their life they must first lose it.

 ### Talk/address/ sermon

Being a disciple means being a learner. God asks us to follow his ways and not our own. Sometimes our calling leads us into places and situations where we may not wish to go. Our Christian life is full of paradoxes, full of opposites which bring us closer to God; to lose, we find; to let go, we keep; to die, we live.

What things in your life could you lose or lay aside which would bring you closer to God?

What activity or situation stops you from taking the next step in your Christian commitment?

What anxieties and fears do we have that need to be presented to God?

Congregational/ group activities

- In groups play Pass the Parcel, but instead of prizes in each layer place a Bible quotation written on a piece of card. Each scriptural passage will tell the reader what is required in being a follower of Jesus. Each layer of the parcel is like a layer of our lives which we are asked by God to take and lay aside for his sake.

- Circle dance. Stand in a circle facing anti-clockwise. Place your left hand on the shoulder of the person in front: this represents the cross we are asked to bear. Place your right hand over your heart: this represents the love we have to offer to God and to those around us. The dance needs slow, meditative music, such as Pachelbel's Canon. In time with the music the circle will begin with the right foot and take three steps forward, and then rock back onto the left foot and repeat, until the music stops. Once the circle has adopted the rhythm, people may be invited to close their eyes and let the dance become a prayerful offering.

- Give everyone one large stick and one small stick (garden canes or tree prunings will do) and a small piece of twine or string.

Ask each person to make a cross with the sticks and tie them together with the string. As they are doing so, ask them to think about the words of Jesus in the reading, and also St Paul's instruction to follow God by sacrificial love. What are the ways in which our love takes us the extra mile? What issues make us stand up and be counted? Think of one thing in which we participate (a relationship, a situation, or an issue) that requires serving others, and perhaps laying aside something of ourselves. When the cross has been made, place it before the altar – perhaps planted in a sand-filled bowl – as your acknowledgement of following God.

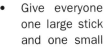

Prayers/ intercessions

The crosses may be used to form the basis of the intercessions.

Several of the crosses can represent areas for prayer:

the Church
the nations
homes and families
our communities
the sick and suffering
the departed.

At the end of each section these words may be said or sung:

Through our lives and by our prayers, your Kingdom come.

'Music', in WGS 1

Alternatively, use one of the following prayers:

'Through our lives and by our prayers', in WGS 1
Prayers for Children (No. 201)

'Christ the hope', and 'My cross', in Geoffry Duncan (ed.), *Dare to Dream,* Fount, 1995 (pp. 130, 179)

Stories and other resources

'Moses hears God's call', in *The Puffin Children's Bible*

'The burning bush', and 'The transfiguration', *The Dorling Kindersley Family Bible,* Dorling Kindersley, 1994

M. Lashbrook, 'Who needs a boat?', in *The Story of Moses,* Candle Books, 1994

'Disciples', in *Pick and Mix* (pp. 52–55)

'The light of God's glory', in *Things To Do In Children's Worship* (p. 33)

'Good neighbours', in *Things To Do In Children's Worship* (p. 67)

Drama:

Episode 4, in *Plays for All Seasons* (p. 88)

 ## Music

Be still and know (WGS 2, p.96)

God it was (WGS 3, p.48)

Jesus is a friend of mine (JP 136)

Take up thy cross (HAMNS 237, HON 465, HTC 114)

Thank you Jesus (SHF 500)

Thank you, Lord, for this new day (HON 468, JP 232)

The God of Abraham praise (HAMNS 331, HON 478, HTC 9, SHF 507)

The head that once was crowned with thorns (HAMNS 141, HON 480, HTC 182)

The voice from the bush (*The Children's Hymn Book* Kevin Mayhew, 1997, 199)

When I needed a neighbour (HON 548)

Collect and Post communion prayer

Advent 1998 to Advent 1999	Thirteenth Sunday after Trinity on p. 134
Advent 2001 to Advent 2002	Fourteenth Sunday after Trinity on p. 134
Advent 2004 to Advent 2005	

Sunday between 4 and 10 September

Proper 18

 ## Readings

Continuous

Exodus 12.1-14

The Lord gives Moses and Aaron instructions to prepare for the Passover. All the people of Israel are to prepare for an event that will finally begin their long progress to freedom and the promised land. It will become a day of remembrance for them as they remember how God has brought them deliverance from the Egyptians.

or Related

Ezekiel 33.7-11

The prophet has been made the sentinel for God and must warn the wicked of the fate that awaits them. He is to warn the house of Israel that they must turn away from their evil ways to escape death.

Romans 13.8-14

Paul repeats Jesus' teaching that all the commandments are summed up in the words 'Love your neighbour as yourself'.

Matthew 18.15-20

Jesus gives clear teaching on dealing with differences amongst believers. If someone is sinned against, they should point it out directly to the person at fault. They should only involve others if the sinner will not listen. Jesus then promises that where two or three are gathered together in his name, he will be present with them.

 ## Talk/address/ sermon

Use the Passover plates from the group activities as a visual aid for the talk.

Ask the congregation to think of a great event that has happened during their lifetime. Interview a member of the congregation who has an interesting story relating to a national event (or alternatively, with some fascinating details of events in the church's life).

For the Jewish people, one of the greatest events that they remember in their history is the Passover. Use the Passover plate to explain what happened to Moses and the Israelite people and why the event was of such importance to them. What events do we celebrate and remember as Christians? Why should these be important to us?

 ## Congregational/ group activities

- Ask the groups to think back to the major events that have occurred in: the world, their country, their church, their family and their own lives. Ask them to draw or write about the main event.

- Begin a poster or banner entitled 'Journey to the Promised Land'. Draw images from the story of the Passover and stick these to the banner or poster. Add more images as you follow the story of Moses and the Israelites through the coming weeks. Alternatively, produce a banner with the words from the Gospel reading, 'Where two or three come together in my name, there am I with them.'

- Give each person two sheets of A4 paper. Ask them to fold these in half, to make an A5 book of eight sides. They should put the title 'My Prayer Diary' on the cover and the names of the days of the week on each of the other pages. What might they be able to pray for on each day of the coming week? They might use the headings: Friends, Family, School/Work, Church, World, the Sick and Myself.

> 'Where two or three come together in my name, there I am with them.'

- The Seder dish is used in many Jewish households as part of the Passover meal. On the Seder dish are placed items of food which are symbols recalling part of the story of how God delivered the children of Israel from slavery in Egypt. These include: matzo or unleavened bread (the bread the children of Israel made when they were in a hurry to leave Egypt); salt water or vinegar, recalling the tears of the slaves; burnt bone as a reminder of the Paschal offering, which used to be made whilst the Temple still stood. Give each group some paper plates, scissors, glue, paper and crayons. Ask them to draw the items that would appear on a Seder plate, cut them out and stick them onto their plate.

Prayers/ intercessions

Place large posters with the headings: 'World', 'Church', 'Family', 'Myself' at the front of the church. During the singing of 'Father, we love you' ask the people to bring their prayers (written in the group activity time) and place these on the appropriate posters.

Use the following prayer:

We bring before God all the events that have happened to us and to our world; all the events that have shaped us and changed us, all the situations that have left us with joy, sorrow or pain.

We pray for the events in our world . . .

As we remember them,

Lord, hear our prayer.

Stories and other resources

'Maximus meets a good Samaritan', in *Short Tails and Tall Stories*

Alan Macdonald, *Whispering in God's Ear*, Lion, 1994

Jill Fuller, *Gazing in Wonder*, Kevin Mayhew, 1996

Prayers for Children

 ## Drama

'Love in the twenty-first century', in *Rap, Rhyme and Reason*

 ## Music

Father God, I wonder (HON 119)

Father, we love you (HON 126)

Forgive our sins as we forgive (HAMNS 362, HON 141, HTC 111)

Inspired by love and anger (*Love and Anger,* Wild Goose Publications, 1997, 44)

Jesus, Jesus, how I adore you (WP 39)

Lord, enthroned in heavenly splendour (HAMNS 263, HON 309, HTC 416, SHF 336)

Love is his word (HON 322)

My God, how wonderful thou art (HAMNS 102, HON 343, HTC 369, SHF 370)

Collect and Post communion prayer

Advent 1998 to Advent 1999	Fourteenth Sunday after Trinity on p. 134
Advent 2001 to Advent 2002	Fifteenth Sunday after Trinity on p. 135
Advent 2004 to Advent 2005	

Sunday between 11 and 17 September

Proper 19

 ## Readings

Continuous

Exodus 14.19-31

As the Israelites flee from the Egyptians, the Lord comes to their aid. A pillar of cloud separates one army from another. Moses stretches out his hand and the Lord parts the Red Sea. After the Israelites have crossed, the waters return and destroy the Egyptians.

or Related

Genesis 50.15-21

Joseph's brothers are fearful that he will exact revenge upon them for their earlier treatment of him. They concoct the story that, before Jacob's death, he asked that their crimes would be forgiven. Joseph promises to provide for them and for their children.

Romans 14.1-12

Paul pleads for believers to refrain from judging each other and thinking themselves better than others. We should not pass judgement on others, or despise them, for we all will stand before the judgement seat of God and are accountable to him for our actions.

Matthew 18.21-35

Peter asks how many times he should forgive another believer who sins against him. Jesus replies that he should not limit forgiveness to seven times but 'seventy-seven times'. He illustrates the need to forgive, by telling the parable of the unforgiving servant.

Talk/address/ sermon

Ask two groups of four people to come up to the front. Give each group several toilet rolls and ask them to choose a volunteer to be completely covered in toilet paper (or use newspapers if you feel adventurous!). See which group can completely cover their volunteer in the shortest possible time. Now ask the volunteers to rip off the paper. What did it feel like to be completely covered up? How did it feel to be able to break free again?

Talk about the reading from Exodus, comparing it to some of the great escape stories of the past. How would the Israelites have felt when the Egyptian army was catching up with them? How would they have felt when they realized they were free, and would no longer need to be slaves?

 ## Congregational/ group activities

- Divide the congregation into groups of three or four. Give each group three ice lolly sticks, felt tip pens and crayons to make stick puppets of the king and two servants in the parable. Give each group a box to decorate (if you can find enough cardboard boxes!) and to prepare the play for the beginning of the talk.

- Continue with the 'Journey to the Promised Land' display or banner, showing the scene of the parting of the Red Sea.

- Discuss the theme of forgiveness in groups. What does it mean to 'be forgiven'? When do we find it difficult to forgive? Give each group pieces of card (perhaps cut out in the shape of a cross). Ask them to write their own prayers onto these.

- Dramatize the Gospel reading in groups of four: one person should read the Bible passage, whilst the others take on the parts of the king and the two servants and mime along to the reading. Alternatively, ask the group to think of a modern-day version of the parable and to act this out for others in the congregation.

- Use the visual aid from the talk in the group activities. Each group should have a toilet roll and choose the smallest child to try to wrap up in the toilet paper in the shortest possible time (as long as the child won't be frightened).

Prayers/intercessions

Use the following responses to begin a time of intercessory prayer:

Incline your ear to me;
be swift to answer when I call.

Incline your ear to me;
be swift to answer when I call.

Lord, hear my prayer,
and let my cry come before you:
be swift to answer when I call.

Hide not your face from me
in the day of my trouble:
be swift to answer when I call.

You, Lord, endure for ever,
and your name from age to age:
be swift to answer when I call.

You will arise and have compassion on Zion,
for it is time to have pity on her:
be swift to answer when I call.

Glory to the Father, and to the Son, and to the Holy Spirit.
Incline your ear to me;
be swift to answer when I call.

Patterns for Worship (p. 117)

Place a large wooden cross by the side of the altar.

During the singing of 'God forgave my sin', ask the congregation to bring up their cross-shaped card and stick their prayers onto the cross (see illustration p. 102).

Stories and other resources

'Account number 54321', in *50 Five Minute Stories*

'Hortense the happy hippo', in *Short Tails and Tall Stories*

Sue Relf, *100 Instant Ideas for All-Age Worship*, Kingsway, 1998

Michael Botting (ed.), 'Joseph', in *Teaching the Family*, Kingsway, 1973

Drama

'Come on cough up!', in *Act One*

'The unforgiving juggler', in *Playing Up*

Music

Amazing grace (HON 27, HTC 28, SHF 10)

Father of heaven, whose love profound (HAMNS 97, HON 124, HTC 359)

God forgave my sin (HON 167, SHF 126)

I love you Lord Jesus (BBP 27)

It's hard to say 'I'm sorry' (BBP 75)

Just as I am, without one plea (HAMNS 246, HON 287, HTC 440, SHF 304)

Lord, forgive me (WP 49)

Collect and Post communion prayer

Advent 1998 to Advent 1999	Fifteenth Sunday after Trinity on p. 135
Advent 2001 to Advent 2002	Sixteenth Sunday after Trinity on p. 135
Advent 2004 to Advent 2005	

Sunday between 18 and 24 September

Proper 20

Readings

Continuous

Exodus 16.2-15

The Israelites complain to Moses that they have been sent from Egypt into a wilderness where they will die of hunger. God sends quails in the evening and manna in the morning to provide for them – but only enough for their immediate needs and never enough to store up for future use.

or Related

Jonah 3.10 – 4.11

This is the conclusion to the story of Jonah. God saves the people of Nineveh from threatened destruction. Jonah is angry that God has allowed them to survive. God allows a plant to grow, to give shade to Jonah in the heat. He then sends a worm to destroy the bush. When Jonah complains again, God compares Jonah's concern for the destruction of a mere plant, to his attitude to the whole city of Nineveh.

Philippians 1.21-30

Paul promises to send Timothy and Epaphroditus to aid the people of Philippi in their faith. He asks them especially to welcome Epaphroditus, as he has risked his life for Christ and for Paul.

Matthew 20.1-16

Jesus compares the kingdom of heaven to a landowner, who hires labourers throughout the day to work in his vineyard. When evening comes, he pays each of the labourers the same amount for their work. Some complain about their 'unfair' treatment. The landowner makes it clear that it is his decision how much he chooses to pay each worker. Jesus concludes the parable with the statement that the last will be first, and the first will be last.

Talk/address/ sermon

Use as a visual aid a poster with the word 'Welcome' written in many different languages. Ask the congregation to think of situations when they have felt isolated and alone.

In the epistle reading, Paul urges the Philippians to welcome his friend Epaphroditus, who he is sending to aid them in their faith. Who was the first person to welcome you into this church? How do we welcome others into God's family – and how can we ensure that all people, whatever their background, language or culture, are welcomed into our church?

Congregational/ group activities

- Continue with the 'Journey to the Promised Land' display or banner. Alternatively, produce a banner with the words 'Sing to him, sing praises to him and speak of all his marvellous works.'

- This is the first week of a series of readings in Philippians. This week the theme is welcoming others. Ask each group to create a welcome poster for the church. Alternatively, ask them to produce a banner that uses the word 'Welcome' in as many languages as possible.

- Give each group information on one of the missionaries or organizations that your church supports. Ask them to write a letter of encouragement for the work that they have been doing.

- 'All about me' sheets. Ask groups to write some information on themselves, to be displayed on the church bulletin board. You might want to give a series of questions for them to answer, such as 'What's their name? What are their big likes and dislikes? What are their favourite foods/hobbies? Why do they come to church?' Take photographs of the church members over the next few weeks and put up these photos alongside the 'All about me' sheets.

Sing to him , sing praises to him and speak of all his marvellous works.

- Send off in advance for material from Christian Aid, Tear Fund, or other Christian charities working in the Third World. Study in depth the needs and history of one particular country. What are their greatest needs? What are the greatest obstacles to justice and fairness in that country? How could our church be involved in helping such a country?

- Play some 'co-operative' party games to show the need to work together to achieve a common goal. Examples of these can be found in Pip Wilson's book *Family Party Games.*

- In groups discuss situations that we face as Christians when we are treated unfairly or unjustly. How can we learn to cope with these? When should we accept our fate patiently and when should we stand up for our rights?

Prayers/ intercessions

Think about the ways that many in the world are treated unfairly and unjustly. Use the posters and material from the Christian charity (that you looked at in the group activities) to pray for a country's particular needs. Use the following prayer to help us realize our own need of forgiveness for treating others unfairly:

Lord God almighty,
We have rejected your law,
And have not obeyed your commandments;
We have ignored the needs of the poor,
And denied justice to the oppressed.

Lord, we have sinned
And dishonoured your holy name:
Have mercy on us;
For Jesus' sake. Amen

Bible Prayers for Worship 7.27 (from Amos 2)

Stories and other resources

Pip Wilson, *Family Party Games*, Marshall Pickering, 1992

Brian Ogden, 'Sometimes the donkey is right', in *Sometimes the Donkey is Right*, Bible Reading Fellowship, 1998

Michael Botting (ed.), 'Jonah', in *Teaching the Family*, Kingsway, 1973

Drama

'A wild time with Kim', in *A Fistful of Sketches*

'Having a whale of a time', in *Act One*

'Everyone gets the same', in *Act One*

 ## Music

Christ's is the world (HON 83)

Heaven shall not wait (HON 207)

King of glory, king of peace (HAMNS 194, HON 288)

Let us praise the Lord our God (BBP 3)

The Lord is king! (HAMNS 107, HON 485, HTC 183, SHF 519)

The love of God (BBP 58)

Through all the changing scenes of life (HAMNS 209, HON 516, HTC 46)

Collect and Post communion prayer

Advent 1998 to Advent 1999	Sixteenth Sunday after Trinity on p. 135
Advent 2001 to Advent 2002	Seventeenth Sunday after Trinity on p. 135
Advent 2004 to Advent 2005	

Sunday between 25 September and 1 October

Proper 21

 ### Readings

Continuous

Exodus 17.1-7

The Israelites complain again to Moses – this time that there is no water for them to drink. The Lord promises to aid them again. He commands Moses to strike his staff against the rock at Horeb, so that water will be provided for his people.

or Related

Ezekiel 18.1-4,25-32

The Lord questions the use of a proverb concerning the land of Israel, 'The parents have eaten sour grapes, and the children's teeth are set on edge'. As far as the Lord is concerned, all lives are his – whether it be the life of the parent or the child – and it is only the person who sins that shall die. Neither are the ways of the Lord unfair. For the wicked shall be saved, if they turn away from their sin and consider God's ways, but those who commit sin shall die for it.

Philippians 2.1-13

Paul urges the people of Philippi to look to the interests of others, rather than themselves. They should follow the example of Jesus who, although he was in the form of God, was prepared to empty himself and be born in human likeness – and to humble himself to die on the cross.

Matthew 21.23-32

The chief priests and elders of the people question Jesus' authority. Jesus silences them by asking them whether they believed the baptism of John came from heaven or was of human origin. He then tells them the parable of two sons: the first refuses to work in his father's vineyard, but later changes his mind. The second promises to work for his father but does not do so.

 ### Talk/address/sermon

As you begin the talk, have a member of the congregation to stand silently behind you and imitate everything that you do. After a while, finally notice them and ask them what they are doing. They point to the Philippians passage and state that Christians should imitate each other. Point out that it is *Christ* that Christians are told to imitate, not fallible clergy or lay leaders! Explain that it is not the outward, but the inward nature of Jesus that we are called to imitate.

Ask the groups to share what they discovered about the character of Jesus from the Philippians reading. Write these points up on a flip-chart or board. Spend a moment of silence reflecting upon the nature of Jesus and the challenge it gives on how each of us should live.

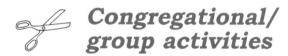 ### Congregational/group activities

- Jesus was a great story-teller, using parables to make a vivid and memorable point. Ask groups to improvise their own stories. The first person in the group begins with a sentence such as 'I was walking out of church this morning when I was astounded to see. . .' Each person in the group contributes a sentence in turn to the story.

- Think of those who are sick or in need in the local community. Write 'Get-well' cards to them.

- Many churches will be celebrating Harvest this week, or over the next few weeks. Give each group a collection of magazines. Ask them to cut out images of all the 'good things' that God gives to us to enjoy. Stick these onto a large piece of card and write in the centre of the collage, 'Thank you, Lord, for all good things you give to us'.

- Study the passage in Philippians. What words are used to describe Jesus? How are we to follow his example?

- What links does the church have with the local school? Interview a foundation governor, teacher or parent about the life of the school. What needs does the school have? How might the church be able to assist and support the work of teachers/governors/parents in the school?

- Continue with the 'Journey to the Promised Land' display or banner showing the scene of Moses striking the rock.

Prayers/ intercessions

Pray for the needs of all the 'carers' in the local community, using the following prayers:

Let your Holy Spirit rest upon all teachers (*insert other caring services here*), Lord,
That they may be guided by you
In thought and word and deed,
And reflect in their lives
Your truth, your patience and your humble love.

Loving Father, Creator of all things,
Author of all goodness, Source of all unifying love,
Make us aware at this moment of your love for us.

Bless our world, our country, our friends, ourselves.
Enrich our leisure, enhance our work,
Make noble our love for others
And grant that at all times and in all places,
In all things great and small, we may do thy perfect will;
Through Jesus Christ our Lord.

Prayers for Children (217 and 224)

Stories and other resources

Brian Ogden, 'Emma and Naaman get better', *Sometimes the Donkey is Right,* Bible Reading Fellowship, 1998

Rick Bundschuh and Tom Finley, *Kick Starters*, Zondervan, 1996

'Big pig is caught in', in *Short Tails and Tall Stories*

Brian Ogden, 'Maximus learns a lesson', in *Maximus Mouse*, Scripture Union, 1991

Prayers for Children, (231 and 232)

 ## Music

All praise to thee, our Lord and King divine (HAMNS 337, HON 18, HTC 204)

Humbly in your sight (WP 30)

I shall praise you, O God (*Love and Anger,* Wild Goose Publications, 1997, 36)

Meekness and majesty (HON 335)

O Jesus, I have promised (HAMNS 235, HON 372, HTC 531, SHF 400)

Praise the Lord! Ye heavens adore him (HAMNS 195, HON 425, HTC 583)

Tell out my soul, the greatness of the Lord (HAMNS 422, HON 467, HTC 42, SHF 498)

There is a Redeemer (HON 500, SHF 534)

Collect and Post communion prayer

Advent 1998 to Advent 1999	Seventeenth Sunday after Trinity on p. 135
Advent 2001 to Advent 2002	Eighteenth Sunday after Trinity on p. 136
Advent 2004 to Advent 2005	

Sunday between 2 and 8 October

Proper 22

Readings

Continuous

Exodus 20.1-4,7-9,12-20

The ten commandments. The Lord gives clear instructions for the way his people should live, based upon the fact that he is the one true God who has brought them out of Egypt and out of slavery.

or Related

Isaiah 5.1-7

This passage is known as the 'song of the vineyard'. Israel is likened to a vine, carefully planted and tended by the Lord. It will be laid waste and overgrown by brambles and thorn-bushes, because of its injustice and wickedness.

Philippians 3.4b-14

Paul views all his worldly successes as nothing compared to what he has gained in Christ. He compares his Christian faith to a race. He sees himself forgetting all that lies behind him, straining towards what is ahead and racing towards the finishing-post to win the prize of God's heavenly call in Christ Jesus.

Matthew 21.33-46

The parable of the wicked tenants. A landowner leases out his vineyard to tenants, who refuse to pay their dues. The landowner's messengers are beaten for their troubles and so he decides to send his son, convinced that they will listen to him. However, they decide to kill him so that the vineyard can be theirs.

Talk/address/ sermon

Prepare a number of the congregation beforehand to help you with this talk. Begin by explaining that you are going to abolish all rules in the world. At this point, a volunteer comes riding up on their cycle/motorbike from the back of church. Your attempt to stop them by holding up a card with a red light on it fails miserably. Their excuse is that you have abolished all rules, so they won't bother taking red lights into account. Continue this theme with a number of other incidents (such as someone stealing your bag or sermon notes!). Explain that many rules have a purpose and help us to live a more enjoyable and less chaotic life. In the same way, God's rules are not meant to be a barrier to an enjoyable life, but to help us to enjoy life to the full.

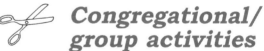 Congregational/ group activities

- Put on a 'mini-olympics', with a mixture of straightforward races and fun games (such as blowing a feather with a newspaper from one end of the room to another).

- Continue with the 'Journey to the Promised Land' display or banner.

- Give each group ten pieces of paper or card and ask them to write out the commandments. Ask them to put them into the correct order – first without looking at the text, and then whilst checking against the passage in Exodus 20.

- Interview a member of the congregation about their own journey of faith. What have been some of the struggles and joys they have faced as a Christian?

 ## Prayers/ intercessions

Use the following prayers, concentrating on hearing God's commandments and obeying them.

The Lord has given us laws to keep:
O Lord, I want to be strong
To obey your commandments,
And to keep them in mind.
Have mercy upon me,
And help me. Amen.

We pray for strength to keep Jesus' commandments:

'Love the Lord your God with all your heart, with all your mind, with all your soul, and with all your strength':
Lord, help us to obey.

'Love your neighbour as yourself':
Lord, help us to obey.

'Love one another as I have loved you':
Lord, help us to obey.

In your mercy strengthen us
And move our hearts to do your will. Amen.

Bible Prayers for Worship 6.2, 6.3

 ## Stories and other resources

David Bell and Terry Clutterham, 'Don't look now', in *Loose the Juice*, CPAS, 1998

Phil Moon, *Keep Taking the Tablets: Repeat Prescription*, CPAS, 1994

'The great gastropod olympics', in *Short Tails and Tall Stories*

 ## Drama

'Christian olympics', in *Plays on the Word*

'The flying Scotsman', in *Playing Up*

 ## Music

Christ is our corner-stone (HAMNS 161, HON 77, HTC 564)

It is a thing most wonderful (HAMNS 70, HON 255, HTC 131)

Marvellous in our eyes (SHF 363)

My song is love unknown (HAMNS 63, HON 346, HTC 136, SHF 378)

Peace, perfect peace, is the gift (HON 414)

Praise to the Holiest in the height (HAMNS 117, HON 426, HTC 140, SHF 450)

The law of the Lord (SHF 514)

Collect and Post communion prayer

Advent 1998 to Advent 1999	Eighteenth Sunday after Trinity on p. 136
Advent 2001 to Advent 2002	Nineteenth Sunday after Trinity on p. 136
Advent 2004 to Advent 2005	

Sunday between 9 and 15 October

Proper 23

Readings

Continuous

Exodus 32.1-14

The people urge Aaron to make gods for them. He forms an image of a calf from their gold and they worship it. Moses intercedes for the people to prevent the Lord from destroying them.

or Related

Isaiah 25.1-9

The prophet extols the majesty of the Lord, who is a refuge to the poor and to the needy in their distress. The prophet looks forward to the time when death itself will be destroyed and all the tears and disgrace of his people will be wiped away forever.

Philippians 4.1-9

Paul urges his fellow believers to stand firm in their faith and always to rejoice in their Lord. They should not worry about anything, but bring all their requests to God, so that they may know his peace – a peace that surpasses all understanding.

Matthew 22.1-14

The parable of the wedding banquet. A king invites guests to his son's wedding banquet, but none will come. In the end he throws wide the invitation to all and punishes those who refused to attend.

 Talk/address/ sermon

Assemble as much party gear as you can (streamers, balloons, party hats and plates, etc.). Ask a group of children to come to the front to help you prepare the church for the party. As they are preparing for the party, give some of the children named invita-tions to members of the congregation. When the children hand these out they discover that no-one wants to come to the party (make sure you have prepared this with the invited people beforehand!). What did it feel like to spend so much time preparing for the party and be turned down? What party is Christ talking about in the reading? Who is invited and how does God feel when people reject him? Ensure the talk ends with a general invitation for all to join in the party at the end of the service.

✂ Congregational/ group activities

- Prepare decorations for the party at the end of the service. Make paper chains, party hats, decorate paper plates, etc.

- Act out the parable of the wedding banquet as a puppet show. Draw the characters of the paper on card. Cut these out and stick them onto lollipop sticks. Put a blanket over several chairs to act as the puppet theatre and practise the play, ready for performance as part of the party.

- Decorate digestive biscuits with coloured icing or make simple chocolate krispie cakes for the party.

Prayers/ intercessions

Pray especially for world issues today. Use these intercessions as a basis for the prayers:

We pray for God's faithfulness to be known in ou world, saying:
faithful God:
glorify your name.

In a world of change and hope,
of fear and adventure;
faithful God:
glorify your name.

In human rebellion and obedience,
in our seeking and our finding;
faithful God:
glorify your name.

In the common life of our society,
in prosperity and need;
faithful God:
glorify your name.

As your church proclaims your goodness
in words and action;
faithful God:
glorify your name.

Among our friends
and in our homes;
faithful God:
glorify your name.

In our times of joy,
in our days of sorrow;
faithful God:
glorify your name.

In our strengths and triumphs,
in our weakness and at our death;
faithful God:
glorify your name.

In your saints in glory
and on the day of Christ's coming;
faithful God:
glorify your name.

Patterns for Worship (p. 81–82)

Stories and other resources

'The squirrel who was afraid of heights', in *Short Tails and Tall Stories*

David Bell and Terry Clutterham, 'Just say Yes!', in *Loose the Juice*, CPAS, 1998

Phil Moon, *Keep Taking the Tablets: Repeat Prescription*, CPAS, 1994

Drama:

'The case of the golden calf', in *Playing Up*

'The banana party', in *Playing Up*

'A little yellow idol', in *Act Two*

Music

Be bold, be strong (JU p. 40)

Bread of heaven, on thee we feed (HAMNS 271, HON 67, HTC 398)

Jesu, lover of my soul (HAMNS 123, HON 261, HTC 438)

Jubilate Deo (BBP 2)

Peace, perfect peace, is the gift (HON 414)

Rejoice! Rejoice! Christ is in you (MP 572)

Rejoice! The Lord is king (HAMNS 139, HON 432, HTC 180, SHF 463)

Collect and Post communion prayer

Advent 1998 to Advent 1999	Nineteenth Sunday after Trinity on p. 136
Advent 2001 to Advent 2002	Twentieth Dunday after Trinity on p. 136
Advent 2004 to Advent 2005	

Sunday between 16 and 22 October

Proper 24

 ## Readings

Continuous

Exodus 33.12-23

Moses pleads that the Lord's presence would clearly be with his people, as they journey towards the promised land. The Lord tells Moses that he will make his glory known to him.

or Related

Isaiah 45.1-7

The Lord has chosen Cyrus to subdue nations and strip kings of their authority. This will be done so that all may know that there is no other god who has such power to do these things.

1 Thessalonians 1.1-10

Paul gives thanks for the church of the Thessalonians because of their steadfast faith and love. Their faith has not only prevailed through persecution but has also spread to other believers in Macedonia and Achaia.

Matthew 22.15-22

The Pharisees plot to entrap Jesus. They ask him whether or not it is lawful to pay taxes to the emperor. Jesus responds by asking them whose portrait it is on a denarius and giving the sound advice that they should give to the emperor the things that are the emperor's, and to God the things that are God's.

Talk/address/ sermon

Have a large backdrop/sheet of card/flip chart/OHP with the word 'Jesus' printed very large across it. Have some other smaller pieces of card available, perhaps six that when put together will cover the first piece. Ask people what is important to them, write these things (money, good job, friends etc.) on the smaller pieces of card and use them to cover the word Jesus until it can't be seen. Relate this to all that can entrap and enslave us, and separate us from Jesus.

Congregational/ group activities

*   Collect together many different coins from different countries. Produce a collage of these (or use coin-rubbings and cut these out and stick them on) to illustrate the gospel reading.

*   Continue with the 'Journey to the Promised Land' banner or poster.

*   Collect together magazines and papers from the last week. Ask the groups to cut out symbols of authority and power. Why do we rely upon these?

What power do they have over us? Is it for good or for evil? What would be Christ's response to this form of authority or power?

- Review the work of Jubilee 2000. How successful has it been in its effort to cancel Third World debt? What work is there still to achieve? How might we as individuals and a Church take forward the vision of Jubilee 2000?

Prayer/ intercessions

Focus prayers this week on the needs of the worldwide and local church, using the following prayer:

We pray that Christ may be seen in the life of the Church, saying:
Jesus, Lord of the Church:
in your mercy, hear us.

You have called us into the family
of those who are the children of God.
May our love for our brothers and sisters in Christ
be strengthened by your grace.
Jesus, Lord of the Church:
in your mercy, hear us.

You have called us to be a temple
where the Holy Spirit can dwell.
Give us clean hands and pure hearts
so that our lives will reflect your holiness.
Jesus, Lord of the Church:
in your mercy, hear us.

You have called us to be a light to the world
so that those in darkness come to you.
May our lives shine as a witness
to the saving grace you have given for all.
Jesus, Lord of the Church:
in your mercy, hear us.

You have called us to be members of your body,
so that when one suffers, all suffer together.

We ask for your comfort and healing power
to bring hope to those in distress.
Jesus, Lord of the Church:

in your mercy, hear us.
You have called us to be the Bride
where you, Lord, are the Bridegroom.
Prepare us for the wedding feast
where we will be united with you for ever.
Jesus, Lord of the Church:
hear our prayer,
and make us one in heart and mind
to serve you with joy for ever. Amen

Patterns for Worship (pp. 80 –81)

Stories and resources

Michael Botting (ed.), 'Moses', in *Teaching the Family*, Kingsway, 1973

'The determined frog', in *The Lion Storyteller Bedtime Book*, Lion, 1998

 # Music

All my hope on God is founded (HAMNS 336, HON 15, HTC 451)

Christ is the King! O friends rejoice (HAMNS 345, HTC 492)

Give thanks with a grateful heart (HON 154)

Immortal, invisible, God only wise (HAMNS 199, HON 242, HTC 21, SHF 210)

Let us sing and praise God for all that he has done (JU p. 16)

My God is so big (JU p. 6)

O worship the Lord in the beauty of holiness (HAMNS 49, HON 394, HTC 344, SHF 429)

Seek ye first (HON 442)

Collect and Post communion prayer

Advent 1998 to Advent 1999	Twentieth Sunday after Trinity on p. 136
Advent 2001 to Advent 2002	Twenty-First Sunday after Trinity on p. 137
Advent 2004 to Advent 2005	

Sunday between 16 and 22 October

Sunday between 23 and 29 October

Proper 25

 ## Readings

Continuous

Deuteronomy 34.1-12

Deuteronomy ends with an account of Moses journeying to Mount Nebo, opposite Jericho, so the Lord can show him the promised land. Moses dies and is succeeded by Joshua.

or Related

Leviticus 19.1-2,15-18

Moses is to tell the people of Israel that they must be holy, just as the Lord is holy. They must treat all with impartiality, love their neighbours and not seek vengeance or bear grudges.

1 Thessalonians 2.1-8

Paul recalls his previous experiences with the church of the Thessalonians. He reminds them that he came in the past, not with words of flattery or seeking praise, but with a deep concern for them and that they should know the gospel.

Matthew 22.34-46

The Pharisees again attempt to entrap Jesus with a difficult theological question – which is the greatest commandment in the law? Jesus replies that the greatest is to love the Lord with all one's heart, soul and mind. The second is to love one's neighbour as oneself. Jesus then poses a theological question of his own, that none dares answer. It also successfully halts any further attempts to entrap him by awkward questions.

Talk/address/ sermon

Run to the front of church holding a large suitcase and dressed as if you are about to go on holiday. Explain how you are just about to leave for your ideal holiday destination. Show all the clothes/passport/money etc. that you have ready for the great trip. A member of the congregation comes with a letter for you. It states that a friend has been taken ill – you decide to give the ticket to someone else and stay behind. Relate this role-play to the reading from Deuteronomy. How would Moses have felt, when God told him he would not enter into the promised land? Why was he not allowed to do so?

Write out the words of Matthew 22 verses 37 and 39 ('Love the Lord your God with all your heart and with all your soul and with all your mind' and 'Love your neighbour as yourself') on separate pieces of card. Give each child a different word from the verses and ask one adult (or older child) to sort the children into the correct order, so that the congregation can read the verses. What does it mean to be a good neighbour?

Congregational/ group activities

- Collect together a number of colour magazines and newspapers. Cut out any pictures that show 'love in action'. Stick these onto a large board to illustrate the Gospel reading.

- Make a chain of figures. Fold a sheet and cut out the figures, to show them linked together, hand in hand. Write the words 'Love your neighbour as yourself' on the chain.

- Think about different people who care for us in our community. How do they show God's love in action? Draw pictures of nurses/firemen/teachers. Think of ways that we can pray for them. Write a prayer and stick this on the pictures.

- Ask the groups to think about verses 37-39 of the Gospel reading. What does it mean to love our neighbours? Ask them to present role-plays of situations when we can help those in need.

- This is the final session on the 'Journey to the Promised Land' poster or banner. Finish the work on this. You might wish to add the words from Leviticus 19.1, 'Be holy because I, the Lord your God, am holy' to your banner/poster.

Prayers/ intercessions

Focus on prayers for each other and for ourselves. Use the following as a basis for the prayers:

Lord Jesus, Teacher,
This is what you want us to learn,
Not the world's wisdom, but God's
And so we pray
Awaken us to our need of you in our lives
And you will give us your life

Move us with sorrow for the sorrow of the world
And you will make us strong through our tears

Give us the humility to admit our failures
And you will bring treasure out of them

Make us hungry for justice
And you will give us food that lasts

Help us to see others through your eyes
And you will show us ourselves with love

Show us how to practise what we preach
And we will see God in everyone

Support us in standing firm for truth, even when it costs
And the truth will also make us free.

'God's wisdom', in *The Pattern of our Days* (p. 161)

Stories and other resources

'Love', in *Pick and Mix* (p. 112)

The Pattern of our Days (p. 161)

Bob Hartman, *Cheer up, Chicken*, Lion, 1998

'Teamwork', in *50 Five Minute Stories*

Drama

'Love is like this', in *Playing Up*

'Lean on me', in A *Fistful of Sketches*

Music

Bind us together, Lord (HON 60, SHF 39)

God's love is deeper than the deepest ocean (JU p. 90)

Hail to the Lord's anointed (HAMNS 142, HON 193, HTC 190, SHF 146)

Help us to help each other (HON 208)

O thou, who camest from above (HAMNS 233, HON 392, HTC 552, SHF 424)

Put thou thy trust (HAMNS 223, HON 429)

The love of God be with you (JU p. 86)

Thy hand, O God, has guided (HAMNS 171, HON 518, HTC 536)

Collect and Post communion prayer

Advent 1998 to Advent 1999	Last Sunday after Trinity on p. 137
Advent 2001 to Advent 2002	
Advent 2004 to Advent 2005	

Bible Sunday

(Bible Sunday may be celebrated in preference to the provision for the Last Sunday after Trinity)

 ## *Readings*

Nehemiah 8.1-4a [5-6] 8-12

The people of Israel gather in the rebuilt city, to hear the scribe Ezra read from the book of the law of Moses. The people weep when they hear the words of the law. However, Nehemiah and the Levites tell them not to grieve, but to take strength in the joy of the Lord.

Colossians 3.12-17

The word of Christ dwells richly in us as we learn to clothe ourselves with God's compassion, kindness, humility, meekness and patience.

Matthew 24.30-35

Jesus tells his disciples of the signs that mark the Second Coming. The final verse is a promise that, even though heaven and earth will pass away, his words will remain forever.

Collect

Blessed Lord,
who caused all holy scriptures
   to be written for our learning:
help us so to hear them,
to read, mark, learn and inwardly digest them
that, through patience, and the comfort of your
   holy word,
we may embrace and for ever hold fast
   the hope of everlasting life,
which you have given us in our Saviour Jesus
   Christ,
who is alive and reigns with you,
in the unity of the Holy Spirit,
one God, now and for ever.

 ## *Talk/address/ sermon*

Ask for some volunteers to help you in moving your 'library' to the front of church. Read from several of these. Can people guess where the readings have been taken from? (All the readings will come from the Bible. Read a variety of texts, including poetry from the psalms, history literature, a parable, and one of the laws from Deuteronomy or Leviticus.) Explain how the Bible is constructed of a series of books, written by different people and in different styles. Place large placards on the floor with headings (such as The Law, History, Wisdom, Prophecy, Gospel, Letters). Give the volunteers the correct number of books (66 in all) to place under the separate headings. Although the Bible consists of many different forms of writing, what themes link these all together?

 ## *Congregational/ group activities*

- Play a game of charades. Each person in turn is given the name of a famous Bible character and must mime what they were famous for. Alternatively, give each group of three or four people a famous event or story to act out. After a quick rehearsal, they should act it out for the others, to see who can guess what scene it is.

- Give each group a sheet of well-known Bible verses – but with the words of each in the wrong order. Can people work out what they are?

- Give each group a sheet of Bible verses (preferably less familiar ones). Alongside these place a jumbled-up list of references. Can people work out which books of the Bible the verses might have come from? How can we work this out (e.g. spotting whether they are poetry/history/laws, who is mentioned in them)?

Prayers/ intercessions

The following responses are particularly suitable for Bible Sunday, but they may be used at other times in the Christian Year.

You have given us your Word in the Bible,
Listen to his Word
Great is your Word.
Great is your love.

You have told us of your love for us.
Experience his love.
Great is your name.
Great is your love.

You have created all things.
Share in his Creation.
Great is your Creation.
Great is your love.

Through the example of Jesus we have learned how to
     live.
Follow his Way.
Great is the Way.
Great is your love.

You died for us on a cruel cross.
Great, so great is your love.

You rose again and live with us.
Alleluia!

Children Celebrate! (p. 33)

Stories and other resources

Betty Pedley and John Muir 'All-Age service for Bible Sunday', *Children in the Church?*, NS/CHP, 1997 (p. 33)

'The Bible', in *Children Celebrate!* (p. 32)

'Bible', in *Pick and Mix* (p. 18)

Michael Botting (ed.), 'Bible Sunday', in *Teaching the Family*, Kingsway, 1973

Drama

'The Adrian Puffin show', in *A Fistful of Sketches*

'The good ol' book', in *Playing Up*

Music

Come, Holy Ghost, our hearts inspire (HAMNS 448, HON 91)

Father of mercies, in thy word (HAMNS 167, HTC 247)

God has spoken – by his prophets (HTC 248)

Inspired by love and anger (HON 252)

Love is his word (HON 322)

May your loving spirit (BBP 45)

Thou whose almighty word (HAMNS 180, HON 514, HTC 506, SHF 554)

You shall go out with joy (HON 571, SHF 641)

Post communion prayer

God of all grace,
your Son Jesus Christ fed the hungry
with the bread of his life
and the word of his kingdom:
renew your people with your heavenly grace,
and in all our weakness
sustain us by your true and living bread;
who is alive and reigns, now and for ever.

Dedication Festival

The First Sunday in October or Last Sunday after Trinity

 ## Readings

1 Kings 8.22-30

Solomon stands before the altar of the Lord and dedicates the newly constructed temple. He extols the majesty of the Lord and remembers the covenant that was made with his people.

or

Revelation 21.9-14

In the vision of the new heaven and new earth, John sees the holy city of Jerusalem – transformed by the glory of God, with a radiance like a very rare jewel.

Hebrews 12.18-24

The writer looks back to the time when the Law was given at Mount Sinai and compares the old and new covenants.

Matthew 21.12-16

Jesus drives out the money changers from the Temple, who have turned the building into a den of thieves rather than a house of prayer. He then displays his own authority by healing the blind and lame who come to him in the Temple.

Collect

Almighty God,
to whose glory we celebrate the dedication
   of this house of prayer:
we praise you for the many blessings
you have given to those who worship you here:
and we pray that all who seek you in this place
    may find you,
and, being filled with the Holy Spirit,
may become a living temple acceptable to you;
through Jesus Christ your Son our Lord,
who is alive and reigns with you,
in the unity of the Holy Spirit,
one God, now and for ever.

Talk/address/ sermon

Bring in posters or pictures of some of the most famous buildings in the world (such as the Taj Mahal or the Pyramids). Why were these built and for whom? Compare the purpose of these buildings with your own church or nearby cathedral. Why were these built and for whom?

Give a group of children a variety of boxes and containers. How high a tower can they construct? What would have given it a firmer foundation? Link this example to the theme of today – of building our lives on the firm foundation of faith in Christ.

 ## Congregational/ group activities

- Give each group two newspapers and a roll of sellotape. How tall a tower can they construct and which is the sturdiest design?

- Find out as much as possible about the different parts of the church building. Why do we have an altar/font/pulpit/vestibules in our church? What are they for and what part do they play in Christian worship?

- A 'house of prayer' card. Give each person a piece of card (about A4 in size), a sheet of paper, some crayons and a pair of scissor. Ask them to write a prayer for someone in need (or draw their picture) in the centre of the card. Cover the prayer with the sheet of paper, divided in half to look like the door of a house. Decorate the rest of the paper to resemble the front of a house.

- Give each group a large cardboard box and a number of sheets of paper, scissors and glue. Each group should write a prayer (or draw their picture) and stick these onto their box, ready for the prayers/intercessions.

Prayers/ intercessions

Assemble together all the boxes from the groups, with their prayers and drawings clearly visible, to make a large wall. Use their prayers during this time of intercession.

Alternatively, use the following prayer to dedicate the church building to God:

Lord, thank you for this building
Where we come for cleansing,
Where we gather round your table,
Where we sing aloud your praise,
Where we proclaim all you have done for us;
Lord, we love the house where you meet us,
The place where your glory dwells:
In the assembly of your people
We stand and praise the Lord! Amen

Bible Prayers for Worship 5.6 (from Psalm 26)

Stories and other resources

'Buildings', in *Pick and Mix* (p. 22)

Nicola Currie and Jean Thomson, 'Solomon's Temple', in *In the Beginning,* NS/CHP, 1995 (p. 63)

Michael Botting (ed.), 'Faith', in *Teaching the Family,* Kingsway, 1973

 ## Music

Colours of day (HON 87, JP 28)

Domine Deus (JU p. 84)

Glorious things of thee are spoken (HAMNS 172, HON 158, HTC 494, SHF 123)

Holy, holy, holy, Lord God almighty (HAMNS 95, HON 212, HTC 7, SHF 168)

Immortal Love, for ever full (HAMNS 133, HON 243, HTC 105)

Jesus, stand among us at the meeting of our lives (HON 279)

Now thank we all our God (HAMNS 205, HON 354, HTC 33)

We are being built into a temple (SHF 567)

Post communion prayer

Father in heaven,
whose Church on earth is a sign of your heavenly
    peace,
an image of the new and eternal Jerusalem:
grant to us in the days of our pilgrimage
that, fed with the living bread of heaven,
and united in the body of your Son,
we may be the temple of your presence,
the place of your glory on earth,
and a sign of your peace in the world;
through Jesus Christ our Lord.

All Saints' Sunday

Sunday between 30 October and 5 November (also The Fourth Sunday Before Advent)

All Saints' Day is celebrated on the Sunday between 30 October and 5 November, or if this is not kept as All Saints' Sunday, on 1 November itself. If you wish to use the collects and readings for the Fourth Sunday before Advent these can be found in *The Christian Year: Calendar, Lectionary and Collects.*

Readings

Revelation 7.9-17

A great multitude stands before the throne and before the Lamb. Together with all the angels and the four living creatures they worship God. The multitude is identified as those that have come through the great ordeal and have washed their robes and made them white in the blood of the Lamb.

1 John 3.1-3

We are now to be called children of God. It has not been fully revealed what we will be. However, we know that when God is revealed we will be like him, for we will see him as he is.

Matthew 5.1-12

The Beatitudes. Jesus teaches his disciples a new way of living that radically changes their way of living – whether they mourn, hunger, or are persecuted for righteousness' sake.

Collect

> Almighty God,
> You have knit together your elect
> In one communion and fellowship
>   in the mystical body of your Son Christ our
>   Lord:
> grant us grace so to follow your blessed saints
> in all virtuous and godly living
> that we may come to those inexpressible joys
> that you have prepared for those who truly love
> you;
> through Jesus Christ your Son our Lord,
> who is alive and reigns with you,
> in the unity of the Holy Spirit,
> one God, now and for ever.

Talk/address/ sermon

Select one or two of the Beatitudes to focus upon in the talk. Hold up the banners produced in the group activities with the Beatitude written out in full. (The example given here is for the verse, 'Blessed are the meek, for they will inherit the earth').

Many have heard these Beatitudes read out many times before. But what do they actually *mean* for us today? Are we expected as Christians to be weak wimps and not care what others do to us? Being meek means trusting God to provide for our needs. It also means being humble and looking after others' interests rather than our own. Who are good examples of 'being meek'? How can I be meek at work/in my family/at church? What difference would it make in my relationships with others?

Congregational/ group activities

- Divide the congregation into groups and give one of the beatitudes to each one. Use the study material from the *Emmaus Growth Book 4: Your kingdom among us* to help each group to look at the particular beatitude in depth. Alternatively, ask each group to produce a large banner, illustrating the beatitude they have been given.

- 'The kingdom is among you'. A series of collages or banners that again address a theme and carry us through the next four weeks. This week the picture is the one from the Revelation of the multitude surrounding the Lamb on the throne. Write out the verse from the passage, 'Salvation belongs to our God who is seated on the throne, and to the Lamb!'

The Kingdom is among you.

- Prepare a child to lead the prayers later in the service.

- Things to praise God for. Give everyone a card with the word Blessings written down the side. They must fill the card in by writing a blessing for each of the letters in the word, e.g. B bedtime stories, L Life etc. Then pray a prayer of thanks for those things. This could also be done as a large group activity.

- The writer of 1 John encourages us to live together as children of God. Think about how we can encourage each other and make a plan to do something this coming week that will encourage someone we know. Write it down and review the plan next week.

Prayers/ intercessions

These prayers can be led by a child if they have had time to prepare during the activities session.

Prayers need to be on OHP or printed on a service sheet.

Child	Lord, when we are worried because we don't think we have enough money.
All	**Remind us, Father, that we are blessed.**
Child	When we are hungry and have no food
All	**Remind us, Father, that we are blessed.**
Child	When we are so upset that we cry

All	**Remind us, Father, that we are blessed.**
Child	When people say that they hate us
All	**Remind us, Father, that we are blessed.**
Child	When we are rich and happy and satisfied
All	**Remind us, Father, that we need you.**

Stories and other resources

S. Cottrell, S. Croft, J. Finney, F. Lawson and R. Warren, *Emmaus Growth Book 4: Your Kingdom Among Us*, NS/CHP, 1998

'Kingdom of God', in *Pick and Mix*

'All Saints', in *Seasons, Saints and Sticky Tape*

'Prayers on winter', in *Prayers for Children* (pp. 180-84)

'All Saints', in *Children Celebrate!* (p. 18)

Drama

Paul Burbridge and Murray Watts, 'A little advice from the Mount', in *The Best Time to Act*, Hodder and Stoughton, 1995

Paul Burbridge and Murray Watts, 'An eye for an eye', in *Lightning Sketches,* Hodder and Stoughton, 1981

'Saints alive', in *Plays for all Seasons*

Music

As we are gathered (HON 40, SHF 24)

Come let us sing of a wonderful love (SHF 67)

For all the saints (HAMNS 305, HON 134, HTC 567)

Help us to help each other, Lord (HON 208)

I sing a song of the saints (JP 115)

Jesus, wher'er thy people meet (HAMNS 162, HON 282, HTC 371)

Soften my heart (MP 606)

Post communion prayer

> God, the source of all holiness
> and giver of all good things:
> may we who have shared at this table
> as strangers and pilgrims here on earth
> be welcomed with all your saints
> > to the heavenly feast on the day of your kingdom;
> through Jesus Christ our Lord.

The Third Sunday Before Advent

Sunday between 6 and 12 November

 ## Readings

Wisdom of Solomon 6.12-16

The beauty of wisdom is described here. She is seen to be radiant and unfading, easily discerned by those who love her and found by those who seek her.

Amos 5.18-24

The festivals, solemn assemblies and burnt-offerings of the people are rejected by the Lord. Instead, they are told to 'let justice roll down like waters and righteousness like an everflowing stream'.

1 Thessalonians 4.13-18

Paul writes about the Second Coming of Christ. The Lord himself will descend from heaven and the dead in Christ will rise first. Then all who are alive will join together with them to meet the Lord and be with him forever.

Matthew 25.1-13

The kingdom of heaven is compared to the wise and foolish bridesmaids. The message is clear: that we should remain vigilant and awake for the coming of the Lord, for we know neither the day nor the hour of his coming.

Collect

Almighty Father,
whose will is to restore all things
in your beloved Son, the king of all:
govern the hearts and minds of those in authority,
and bring the families of the nations,
divided and torn apart by the ravages of sin,
to be subject to his just and gentle rule;
who is alive and reigns with you,
in the unity of the Holy Spirit,
one God, now and for ever.

 ## Talk/address/sermon

Pre-pack a suitcase with clothes etc. as if you were going away on holiday and, as you unpack, ask the congregation what sort of things they take on holiday with them. This can be quite amusing with creative suitcase contents! Talk about what we need to travel by plane or train. Preparing for a big event, such as a family holiday, takes a long time. We need to spend time preparing and making sure all is ready.

Alternatively, ask if anyone saw a TV programme the other night because you missed it. Talk about how frustrating it is to miss something that you have been waiting to see – the next episode of Coronation Street perhaps. Talk about the parable of the wise and foolish bridesmaids. How much worse it must be not to be ready for the biggest event of all time – the return of Jesus. How can we make sure that we are ready for him when he returns?

 ## Congregational/group activities

- 'The kingdom is among you'. This week in the series the banner is about the Second Coming. Draw a picture of the parable of the wise and foolish bridesmaids.

- Get everyone to complete an 'All About Me' questionnaire (my favourite food is . . . I really can't stand . . . (not a person!)). Then in small groups use the questionnaires to introduce each other to the rest of the group. Gather the questions in and ask people at random e.g. 'Fred, what is Ann's goldfish called?' Fred probably won't know the answer – especially if he wasn't in Ann's group. Explain that we can't know everything about each other, and indeed, we shouldn't try to – there is no need because God does know everything about everybody.

- Make a strip of paper into a circle and staple it together. Get everyone to prove that you can't draw a line along both sides without lifting the pen from the paper. So they have to stop and start again. Now make new strips of paper into circles, this time with a single twist in them (mobius strips) and do the same thing again. Explain that in the same way, God's love for us is never ending and life on earth is like the first strip, it is finite, but eternal life is like the second strip and goes on and on.

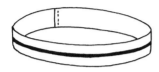

- Give everyone a sheet of paper. Ask them to imagine they had to leave in a hurry from their house and only had time to take five things with them. Ask them to draw or write the names of these five things. Why are these things special to them?

- Review the 'encouragement' plans from last week if you undertook that activity – did anyone get the opportunity to carry out their plan and if so, how did it go.

Prayers/intercessions

These prayers can be led by a child if they have had a chance to prepare during the earlier activity session. The prayers need to be put onto an overhead projector or printed in the service sheets.

Child   Lord, when someone accuses us of something that we have not done,

All   **Thank you that you see us and know us.**

Child   When something hurts too much to talk about,

All   **Thank you that you see us and know us.**

Child   When no-one wants to listen to what we have to say,

All   **Thank you that you see us and know us.**

Child   When we are really sorry but don't get a chance to say so,

All   **Thank you that you see us and know us.**

Child   When we work as hard as we can and nobody praises us,

All   **Thank you that you see us and know us.**

Child   When we don't want to say how scared we are,

All   **Thank you that you see us and know us.**

Child   Heavenly Father, thank you that you see us and know us. We know that we can never be alone when we are hurting and we are sorry when we hurt you. **Amen**

Stories and other resources

Lois Rock, *Words of Gold*, Lion, 1997

'Kingdom of God', in *Pick and Mix*

Compiled by Lisa Potts, *Thank you God: A Book of Children's Prayers*, Hodder and Stoughton, 1997

Drama

Paul Burbridge and Murray Watts, 'Getting ready', in *The Best Time to Act*, Hodder and Stoughton, 1995

Steve and Janet Stickley, 'Action replay', in *Footnotes*, Hodder and Stoughton, 1987

Music

Battle hymn (SHF 540)

Be thou my vision (HAMNS 343, HON 56, HTC 545, SHF 38)

Come, Lord Jesus, come (JU p. 88)

Glory to God, Glory to God (HON 161, JU p. 78)

Love divine, all loves excelling (HAMNS 131, HON 321, HTC 217, SHF 353)

Prepare the way (SHF 457)

Ye servants of the Lord (HAMNS 150, HON 566, HTC 353, SHF 628)

Post communion prayer

God of peace,
whose Son Jesus Christ proclaimed the kingdom
and restored the broken to wholeness of life:
look with compassion on the anguish of the world,
and by your healing power
make whole both people and nations;
through our Lord and Saviour Jesus Christ.

The Second Sunday Before Advent

Sunday between 13 and 19 November

Readings

Zephaniah 1.7,12-18

The coming judgement of the Lord is fast approaching. It will be a bitter day for many, for they have sinned against him. Neither their silver nor their gold will be able to save them from the day of the Lord's wrath.

1 Thessalonians 5.1-11

The day of the Lord will come like a thief in the night. As we are children of light, we are urged not to fall asleep as others do, but keep awake and ready for the coming of the Lord.

Matthew 25.14-30

The parable of the talents. A master gives three slaves differing amounts of money before he leaves on a journey. On the master's return, two are seen to have used the money wisely, and are rewarded by their master. The third is seen as wicked and lazy, by not using the little that he had been given.

Collect

Heavenly Father,
whose blessed Son was revealed
    to destroy the works of the devil
and to make us the children of God and heirs
of eternal life:
grant that we, having this hope,
may purify ourselves even as he is pure;
that when he shall appear in power and great glory
we may be made like him
in his eternal and glorious kingdom;
where he is alive and reigns with you,
in the unity of the Holy Spirit,
one God, now and for ever.

Talk/address/sermon

Christmas is only six weeks away and we are already beginning to think about what to buy people for gifts. Invite one person up (adult or child) and ask them to give you a pre-packed gift which you open. Act as if it is something you always wanted but don't say 'thank you' to the giver. Ask the congregation what is wrong and how they feel when someone doesn't say thank you for something. Explain that we need to say thank you to God too for the things that He has given to us.

Ask one or more of the groups to come to the front and to present their dramatized version of the Gospel reading. God has given each of us talents, or gifts, that we can use in his service. What kinds of gifts does God give us? What can we do to share our gifts with others?

Congregational/group activities

- Divide the congregation into groups of four. Ask them to choose one of the parts from the parable of the talents – the master, or one of the slaves. Narrate the story, whilst the groups mime the actions.

- 'The kingdom is among us' series. Continue making the banner/collage, this week either depicting the parable of the talents, or illustrating the reading from 1 Thessalonians, that the day of the Lord will come 'like a thief in the night'.

- Everyone has a piece of paper and draws something on it that they would like to say thank you to God for. They then show the rest of the group who try to guess what the thing is. Alternatively use mime to illustrate this.

- Group discussion: give each person in the group a fake promissory note for a hundred pounds. How could they use this to further God's work: could they think of a creative way to raise money, or would they invest it in missionary work? How can we best use the talents that the group have been given?

Prayers/intercessions

Use the following prayer:

Father, sometimes we don't want to work hard.

Sometimes it is easier not to help someone, not to do the things that we should do.

Sometimes Lord we would rather listen to some music than listen to a friend in need.

Sometimes we would rather watch television than watch over an ill person.

Sometimes we would rather have a snack than prepare a meal.

Sometimes we would rather pretend that we didn't see an injustice rather than do something about it.

Sometimes we would rather give up than keep on trying.

Sometimes Lord, wouldn't you rather turn away than keep on loving us?

Praise you that you are perfect and we are not.

Amen

Stories and other resources

Prayers for Children ('Praise the Lord' (p. 21) 'Winter' (p. 180))

'Gifts', in *Pick and Mix*

Brian Ogden, 'Picnic in the park', in *Sometimes the Donkey is Right*, Bible Reading Fellowship, 1998

Drama

'Nearly ready', in *Scenes and Wonders*

'The parable of the talents', in *Children Aloud!*

'What have you done with my money?', in *Act One*

Music

God Is Good (SHF 131)

O God, our help in ages past (HAMNS 99, HON 366, HTC 37)

Praise God from whom all blessings flow (HON 417, SHF 436,)

Seek ye first (HON 442, SHF 471)

Soldiers of the cross, arise (HTC 534)

Soldiers of Christ, arise (SHF 483)

We are marching in the light of God (JU p. 34)

Post communion prayer

Gracious Lord,
in this holy sacrament
you give substance to our hope:
bring us at the last
to that fullness of life for which we long;
through Jesus Christ our Saviour.

Christit the King

Sunday between 20 and 26 November (also The Sunday Next Before Advent)

 ### Readings

Ezekiel 34.11-16,20-24

As shepherds seek out their flocks when they are among their scattered sheep, so the Lord will gather together his people from the countries and bring them into their own land. The Lord God will seek the lost and bring back those who have strayed.

Ephesians 1.15-23

Paul continually gives thanks and remembers the people of Ephesus in his prayers, because of their faith in the Lord Jesus. He then prays that they will know the hope and the immeasurable greatness of Jesus' power.

Matthew 25.31-46

The Son of Man will come in glory and all nations will gather before him. On his right hand will be the sheep – the ones who are blessed by God, because they remembered those who suffered. On his left hand will be the goats – those who are cursed, because they did not care for those in need.

Collect

Eternal Father,
whose Son Jesus Christ ascended to the throne
   of heaven
     that he might rule over all things as Lord and
     King:
keep the Church in the unity of the Spirit
and in the bond of peace,
and bring the whole created order to worship at
   his feet;
who is alive and reigns with you,
in the unity of the Holy Spirit,
one God, now and for ever.

Talk/address/ sermon

As this is the last Sunday in the Church's year, review all the main festivals that have occurred in the past year. Illustrate these with the appropriate colours for each season of the Christian year, or with photographs of church events that have taken place. Interview a member of the congregation on their memories of the past year. What has happened to them during the year? How have they felt God's presence with them, or seen him at work in their life?

 ### Congregational/ group activities

- 'The kingdom is among you'. Give each person a piece of paper or card and ask them to draw their own face. Use these pictures as the border for the banner/collage. As this is the last in the series the edges of the banner/collage can be tidied up and any extra work needed can be done on the heading. Make sure that all those who helped to make it have their names on the piece of art somewhere and display it prominently in the Church.

- On a prayer card write a list of things that can get in the way between us and God. Decorate the card and use it as a part of prayer time to remind us that God is more important.

- Using the image of the Cross as a bridge between us and God. Have pictures to complete and colour that show us and God on one side and worldly things on the other (magazine cut-outs perhaps?).

- Make a huge gold crown from cardboard, and ask the children to decorate it 'fit for a king'. Paint 'Christ the King' around the outside and if at all possible, suspend it from somewhere in the Church where it will be visible.

- Make 'Advent' biscuits if you have cooking facilities. If at all possible it is nice to do this for the whole congregation. The idea is that the children in four groups make a large batch of biscuits for each of the Sundays in Advent for the congregation to have at coffee time. They can use cutters in order to have different shapes for each week. This draws the congregation into the children's excitement and anticipation of Christmas and helps the children to feel that they have given something.

Prayers/intercessions

Give everyone a piece of paper in the shape of a crown. Ask everyone to write a short prayer on it and come forward and place it in the centre of a parachute (a large double sheet will do if you don't have a 'chute) held by some children. When all the prayers are in:

Leader   Lord we all have so much to say 'thank you' for, to ask you for, and to say sorry for.

All   Merciful Father, accept these prayers for the sake of your Son, our Saviour and our King. Amen.

Then mushroom the parachute up and the prayers will fly up and flutter down again. This symbolism is enhanced if the children then gather the prayers and stick them on a prayer board in silence.

Alternatively, use the following prayer on the kingship of Christ:

Lord, you are the king, and we tremble before you; you are enthroned in the presence of your people: let everyone praise your great and majestic name:

Holy, holy, the Lord our God is holy!

Our mighty king, you love all that is good; you bring to us truth and justice – our Lord God, we praise you and worship before your throne:

Holy, holy, the Lord our God is holy!

Our Lord God, you answer your people when they pray to you; you speak to us, and give us your laws to obey; you show you are a God who forgives. Our Lord God, we praise you, and come together to worship you;

Holy, holy, the Lord our God is holy!

Bible Prayers for Worship 5.12
(based on Psalm 99)

Stories and other resources

More Things to Do in Children's Worship (pp. 30, 37, 80)

'Winter', in *Prayers for Children*, (p. 180)

100 Instant Children's Talks (pp. 34, 36, 88, 90)

Michael Botting (ed.), 'Which king?', in *Teaching the Family*, Kingsway, 1973

 ## Drama

Paul Burbridge and Murray Watts, 'The newcomer', in *The Best Time to Act*, Hodder and Stoughton, 1995

'Nancy's nightmare', in *Act Two*

 ## Music

Crown him with many crowns (HAMNS 147, HON 103, HTC 174, SHF 75)

Deck thyself, my soul, with gladness (HAMNS 257, HON 108, HTC 400)

Jesus, remember me (HON 276)

King of kings (SHF 43)

Let all mortal flesh keep silence (HAMNS 256, HON 295, HTC 61)

The King is among us (HON 483, SHF 511)

The King of love my shepherd is (HAMNS 126, HON 484, HTC 44, SHF 513)

You are the King of glory (HON 570, SHF 630)

You laid aside your majesty (SHF 638)

Post communion prayer

Stir up, O Lord,
the wills of your faithful people;
that they, plenteously bringing forth the fruit of
   good works,
may by you be plenteously rewarded;
through Jesus Christ our Lord.

Appendix A

Collects and Post Communion Prayers
Ordinary Time (Before Lent)

The following prayers will be used with the Proper 1, 2 or 3 services. Please see the tables on these Sundays to match the collects and post communion prayers with the correct services.

The Fifth Sunday Before Lent

Collect

Almighty God,
by whose grace alone we are accepted
    and called to your service:
strengthen us by your Holy Spirit
and make us worthy of our calling;
through Jesus Christ your Son our Lord,
who is alive and reigns with you,
in the unity of the Holy Spirit,
one God, now and for ever.

Post communion prayer

God of truth,
we have seen with our eyes
    and touched with our hands the bread of life:
strengthen our faith
that we may grow in love for you and for each other;
through Jesus Christ our Lord.

The Fourth Sunday Before Lent

Collect

O God,
you know us to be set
in the midst of so many and great dangers,
that by reason of the frailty of our nature
we cannot always stand upright:
grant to us such strength and protection
as may support us in all dangers
and carry us through all temptations;
through Jesus Christ your Son our Lord,
who is alive and reigns with you,
in the unity of the Holy Spirit,
one God, now and for ever.

Post communion prayer

Go before us, Lord, in all we do
with your most gracious favour,
and guide us with your continual help,
that in all our works
begun, continued and ended in you,
we may glorify your holy name,
and finally by your mercy receive everlasting life;
through Jesus Christ our Lord.

The Third Sunday Before Lent

Collect

Almighty God,
who alone can bring order
to the unruly wills and passions of sinful humanity:
give your people grace
so to love what you command
and to desire what you promise,
that, among the many changes of this world,
our hearts may surely there be fixed
where true joys are to be found;
through Jesus Christ your Son our Lord,
who is alive and reigns with you,
in the unity of the Holy Spirit,
one God, now and for ever.

Post communion prayer

Merciful Father,
who gave Jesus Christ to be for us the bread of life,
that those who come to him should never hunger:
draw us to the Lord in faith and love,
that we may eat and drink with him
at his table in the kingdom,
where he is alive and reigns, now and for ever.

Appendix B

Collects and Post Communion Prayers
Ordinary Time
(After Trinity and Before Advent)

The First Sunday After Trinity

Collect

O God,
the strength of all those who put their trust in you,
mercifully accept our prayers
and, because through the weakness of our mortal
   nature
we can do no good thing without you,
grant us the help of your grace,
that in the keeping of your commandments
we may please you both in will and deed;
through Jesus Christ your Son our Lord,
who is alive and reigns with you,
in the unity of the Holy Spirit,
one God, now and for ever.

Post communion prayer

Eternal Father,
we thank you for nourishing us
with these heavenly gifts:
may our communion strengthen us in faith,
build us up in hope,
and make us grow in love;
for the sake of Jesus Christ our Lord.

The Second Sunday After Trinity

Collect

Lord, you have taught us
that all our doings without love are nothing worth:
send your Holy Spirit
and pour into our hearts that most excellent gift of
   love,
the true bond of peace and of all virtues,
without which whoever lives is counted dead before
   you.
Grant this for your only Son Jesus Christ's sake,
who is alive and reigns with you,
in the unity of the Holy Spirit,
one God, now and for ever.

Post communion prayer

Loving Father,
we thank you for feeding us at the supper of your Son:
sustain us with your Spirit,
that we may serve you here on earth
until our joy is complete in heaven,
and we share in the eternal banquet
with Jesus Christ our Lord.

The Third Sunday After Trinity

Collect

Almighty God,
you have broken the tyranny of sin
and have sent the Spirit of your Son into our hearts
 whereby we call you Father:
give us grace to dedicate our freedom to your service,
that we and all creation may be brought
 to the glorious liberty of the children of God;
through Jesus Christ your Son our Lord,
who is alive and reigns with you,
in the unity of the Holy Spirit,
one God, now and for ever.

Post communion prayer

O God, whose beauty is beyond our imagining
and whose power we cannot comprehend:
show us your glory as far as we can grasp it,
and shield us from knowing more than we can bear
until we may look upon you without fear;
through Jesus Christ our Saviour.

The Fourth Sunday After Trinity

Collect

O God, the protector of all who trust in you,
without whom nothing is strong, nothing is holy:
increase and multiply upon us your mercy;
that with you as our ruler and guide
we may so pass through things temporal
that we lose not our hold on things eternal;
grant this, heavenly Father,
for our Lord Jesus Christ's sake,
who is alive and reigns with you,
in the unity of the Holy Spirit,
one God, now and for ever.

Post communion prayer

Eternal God,
comfort of the afflicted and healer of the broken,
you have fed us at the table of life and hope:
teach us the ways of gentleness and peace,
that all the world may acknowledge
the kingdom of your Son Jesus Christ our Lord.

The Fifth Sunday After Trinity

Collect

Almighty and everlasting God,
by whose Spirit the whole body of the Church
 is governed and sanctified:
hear our prayer which we offer for all your faithful
 people,
that in their vocation and ministry
they may serve you in holiness and truth
to the glory of your name;
through our Lord and Saviour Jesus Christ,
who is alive and reigns with you,
in the unity of the Holy Spirit,
one God, now and for ever.

Post communion prayer

Grant, O Lord, we beseech you,
that the course of this world may be so peaceably
 ordered by your governance,
that your Church may joyfully serve you
 in all godly quietness;
through Jesus Christ our Lord.

The Sixth Sunday After Trinity

Collect

Merciful God,
you have prepared for those who love you
such good things as pass our understanding:
pour into our hearts such love toward you
that we, loving you in all things and above all things,
may obtain your promises,
which exceed all that we can desire;
through Jesus Christ your Son our Lord,
who is alive and reigns with you,
in the unity of the Holy Spirit,
one God, now and for ever.

Post communion prayer

God of our pilgrimage,
you have led us to the living water:
refresh and sustain us
as we go forward on our journey,
in the name of Jesus Christ our Lord.

The Seventh Sunday After Trinity

Collect

Lord of all power and might,
the author and giver of all good things:
graft in our hearts the love of your name,
increase in us true religion,
nourish us with all goodness,
and of your great mercy keep us in the same;
through Jesus Christ your Son our Lord,
who is alive and reigns with you,
in the unity of the Holy Spirit,
one God, now and for ever.

Post communion prayer

Lord God, whose Son is the true vine and the source
    of life,
ever giving himself that the world may live:
may we so receive within ourselves
    the power of his death and passion
that, in his saving cup,
we may share his glory and be made perfect in his
    love;
for he is alive and reigns, now and for ever.

The Eighth Sunday After Trinity

Collect

Almighty Lord and everlasting God,
we beseech you to direct, sanctify and govern
    both our hearts and bodies
in the ways of your laws
    and the works of your commandments;
that through your most mighty protection, both here
    and ever,
we may be preserved in body and soul;
through our Lord and Saviour Jesus Christ,
who is alive and reigns with you,
in the unity of the Holy Spirit,
one God, now and for ever.

Post communion prayer

Strengthen for service, Lord,
the hands that have taken holy things;
may the ears which have heard your word
    be deaf to clamour and dispute;
may the tongues which have sung your praise
    be free from deceit;
may the eyes which have seen the tokens of your love
    shine with the light of hope;
and may the bodies which have been fed with your
    body be refreshed with the fullness of your life;
glory to you for ever.

The Ninth Sunday After Trinity

Collect

Almighty God,
who sent your Holy Spirit
to be the life and light of your Church:
open our hearts to the riches of your grace,
that we may bring forth the fruit of the Spirit
in love and joy and peace;
through Jesus Christ your Son our Lord,
who is alive and reigns with you,
in the unity of the Holy Spirit,
one God, now and for ever.

Post communion prayer

Holy Father,
who gathered us here around the table of your Son
to share this meal with the whole household of God:
in that new world
    where you reveal the fullness of your peace,
gather people of every race and language
    to share in the eternal banquet
    of Jesus Christ our Lord.

The Tenth Sunday After Trinity

Collect

Let your merciful ears, O Lord,
be open to the prayers of your humble servants;
and that they may obtain their petitions
make them to ask such things as shall please you;
through Jesus Christ your Son our Lord,
who is alive and reigns with you,
in the unity of the Holy Spirit,
one God, now and for ever.

Post communion prayer

God of our pilgrimage,
you have willed that the gate of mercy
should stand open for those who trust in you:
look upon us with your favour
that we who follow the path of your will
may never wander from the way of life;
through Jesus Christ our Lord.

The Eleventh Sunday After Trinity

Collect

O God, you declare your almighty power
most chiefly in showing mercy and pity:
mercifully grant to us such a measure of your grace,
that we, running the way of your commandments,
may receive your gracious promises,
and be made partakers of your heavenly treasure;
through Jesus Christ your Son our Lord,
who is alive and reigns with you,
in the unity of the Holy Spirit,
one God, now and for ever.

Post communion prayer

Lord of all mercy,
we your faithful people have celebrated that one true
    sacrifice
    which takes away our sins and brings pardon and
    peace:
by our communion
keep us firm on the foundation of the gospel
and preserve us from all sin;
through Jesus Christ our Lord.

The Twelfth Sunday After Trinity

Collect

Almighty and everlasting God,
you are always more ready to hear than we to pray
and to give more than either we desire or deserve:
pour down upon us the abundance of your mercy,
forgiving us those things of which our conscience is
   afraid
and giving us those good things
   which we are not worthy to ask
but through the merits and mediation
of Jesus Christ your Son our Lord,
who is alive and reigns with you,
in the unity of the Holy Spirit,
one God, now and for ever.

Post communion prayer

God of all mercy,
in this eucharist you have set aside our sins
and given us your healing:
grant that we who are made whole in Christ
may bring that healing to this broken world,
in the name of Jesus Christ our Lord.

The Thirteenth Sunday After Trinity

Collect

Almighty God,
who called your Church to bear witness
that you were in Christ reconciling the world to
   yourself:
help us to proclaim the good news of your love,
that all who hear it may be drawn to you;
through him who was lifted up on the cross,
and reigns with you in the unity of the Holy Spirit,
one God, now and for ever.

Post communion prayer

God our Creator,
you feed your children with the true manna,
the living bread from heaven:
let this holy food sustain us through our earthly
   pilgrimage
until we come to that place
   where hunger and thirst are no more;
through Jesus Christ our Lord.

The Fourteenth Sunday After Trinity

Collect

Almighty God,
whose only Son has opened for us
a new and living way into your presence:
give us pure hearts and steadfast wills
to worship you in spirit and in truth;
through Jesus Christ your Son our Lord,
who is alive and reigns with you,
in the unity of the Holy Spirit,
one God, now and for ever.

Post communion prayer

Lord God, the source of truth and love,
keep us faithful to the apostles' teaching and fellowship,
united in prayer and the breaking of bread,
and one in joy and simplicity of heart,
in Jesus Christ our Lord.

The Fifteenth Sunday After Trinity

Collect

God, who in generous mercy sent the Holy Spirit
   upon your Church in the burning fire of your love:
grant that your people may be fervent
   in the fellowship of the gospel
that, always abiding in you,
they may be found steadfast in faith and active in
   service;
through Jesus Christ your Son our Lord,
who is alive and reigns with you,
in the unity of the Holy Spirit,
one God, now and for ever.

Post communion prayer

Keep, O Lord, your Church,
   with your perpetual mercy;
and, because without you our human frailty cannot but
   fall,
keep us ever by your help from all things hurtful,
and lead us to all things profitable to our salvation;
through Jesus Christ our Lord.

The Sixteenth Sunday After Trinity

Collect

O Lord, we beseech you mercifully to hear the prayers
   of your people who call upon you;
and grant that they may both perceive and know
   what things they ought to do,
and also may have grace and power
   faithfully to fulfil them;
through Jesus Christ your Son our Lord,
who is alive and reigns with you,
in the unity of the Holy Spirit,
one God, now and for ever.

Post communion prayer

Almighty God,
you have taught us through your Son
that love is the fulfilling of the law:
grant that we may love you with our whole heart
and our neighbours as ourselves;
through Jesus Christ our Lord.

The Seventeenth Sunday After Trinity

Collect

Almighty God,
you have made us for yourself,
and our hearts are restless till they find their rest in
   you:
pour your love into our hearts and draw us to yourself,
and so bring us at last to your heavenly city
where we shall see you face to face;
through Jesus Christ your Son our Lord,
who is alive and reigns with you,
in the unity of the Holy Spirit,
one God, now and for ever.

Post communion prayer

Lord, we pray that your grace
   may always precede and follow us,
and make us continually to be given to all good works;
through Jesus Christ our Lord.

The Eighteenth Sunday After Trinity

Collect

Almighty and everlasting God,
increase in us your gift of faith
that, forsaking what lies behind
and reaching out to that which is before,
we may run the way of your commandments
and win the crown of everlasting joy;
through Jesus Christ your Son our Lord,
who is alive and reigns with you,
in the unity of the Holy Spirit,
one God, now and for ever.

Post communion prayer

We praise and thank you, O Christ, for this sacred
    feast:
for here we receive you,
here the memory of your passion is renewed,
here our minds are filled with grace,
and here a pledge of future glory is given,
when we shall feast at that table where you reign
with all your saints for ever.

The Nineteenth Sunday After Trinity

Collect

O God, forasmuch as without you
we are not able to please you;
mercifully grant that your Holy Spirit
may in all things direct and rule our hearts;
through Jesus Christ your Son our Lord,
who is alive and reigns with you,
in the unity of the Holy Spirit,
one God, now and for ever.

Post communion prayer

Holy and blessed God,
you have fed us with the body and blood of your Son
and filled us with your Holy Spirit:
may we honour you,
not only with our lips
but in lives dedicated to the service
    of Jesus Christ our Lord.

The Twentieth Sunday After Trinity

Collect

God, the giver of life,
whose Holy Spirit wells up within your Church:
by the Spirit's gifts equip us to live the gospel of Christ
    and make us eager to do your will,
that we may share with the whole creation
    the joys of eternal life;
through Jesus Christ your Son our Lord,
who is alive and reigns with you,
in the unity of the Holy Spirit,
one God, now and for ever.

Post communion prayer

God our Father,
whose Son, the light unfailing,
has come from heaven to deliver the world
    from the darkness of ignorance:
let these holy mysteries open the eyes of our under-
    standing
that we may know the way of life,
and walk in it without stumbling;
through Jesus Christ our Lord.

The Twenty-First Sunday After Trinity

Collect

Grant, we beseech you, merciful Lord,
to your faithful people pardon and peace,
that they may be cleansed from all their sins
and serve you with a quiet mind;
through Jesus Christ your Son our Lord,
who is alive and reigns with you,
in the unity of the Holy Spirit,
one God, now and for ever.

Post communion prayer

Father of light,
in whom is no change or shadow of turning,
you give us every good and perfect gift
and have brought us to birth by your word of truth:
may we be a living sign of that kingdom
where your whole creation will be made perfect
    in Jesus Christ our Lord.

The Last Sunday After Trinity

Collect

Blessed Lord,
who caused all holy scriptures
    to be written for our learning:
help us so to hear them,
to read, mark, learn and inwardly digest them
that, through patience, and the comfort of your holy
    word,
we may embrace and for ever hold fast
    the hope of everlasting life,
which you have given us in our Saviour Jesus Christ,
who is alive and reigns with you,
in the unity of the Holy Spirit,
one God, now and for ever.

Post communion prayer

God of all grace,
your Son Jesus Christ fed the hungry
with the bread of his life
and the word of his kingdom:
renew your people with your heavenly grace,
and in all our weakness
sustain us by your true and living bread;
who is alive and reigns, now and for ever.

Best-selling drama from The National Society and Church House Publishing

Playing Up
Dave Hopwood

New drama
for 1998
£6.95

Acting up
Dave Hopwood

Even more drama
material by
Dave Hopwood
£5.95

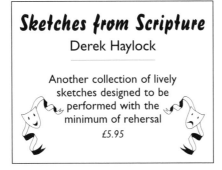

Sketches from Scripture
Derek Haylock

Another collection of lively
sketches designed to be
performed with the
minimum of rehersal
£5.95

Plays on the Word
Derek Haylock

Nineteen fast-moving,
Bible-based sketches,
including eight for
Christmas
£5.95

Plays for all Seasons
Derek Haylock

A collection of 21 dramas
and plays covering
the whole
Christian year
£6.95

A Fistful of Sketches
Dave Hopwood

A wealth of sketches
by the ever-popular
Dave Hopwood
£5.95

All titles above are available from your local Christian bookshop.

The National Society (Church of England) for Promoting Religious Education supports everyone involved in Christian education – teachers, school governors, students, parents, clergy, parish and diocesan education teams – with its legal and professional advice, the resources of its RE centres, courses, conferences and archives.

It is a voluntary Anglican society, also operating ecumenically, and helps to promote inter-faith education and dialogue through its RE centres.

For more details of the Society, or a copy of our current resources catalogue or details on how you can support the continuing work of the Society, please call 0171-222-1672 or email: info@natsoc.org.uk